I AM WORTHY

The Power of Living Without Condemnation

BY CHRIS GRANT

Copyright © 2015 Chris Grant. All rights reserved.

No parts of this book may be used or reproduced by any means, graphic, electronic, or mechanical, including photocopying, recording, taping or by any information storage retrieval system without the written permission of the author except in the case of brief quotations embodied in critical articles and reviews.

This book may be ordered through booksellers or by contacting:

iGlobal Educational Services, LLC
PO Box 7404
Round Rock, Texas 78683-7404
www.iglobaleducation.com
512-761-5898

Because of the dynamic nature of the Internet, any web addresses or links contained in this book may have changed since publication and may no longer be valid. The views expressed in this work are solely those of the author and do not necessarily reflect the views of the publisher, and the publisher hereby disclaims any responsibility for them.

I am Worthy: The Power of Living Without Condemnation

ISBN-13: 978-09882271-9-4

ISBN-10: 0988227193

Book Titles By Chris Grant

I AM WORTHY:
The Power of Living Without Condemnation

USE YOUR HEAD

Note: Check Chris Grant's Personal Website for his latest work at

www.thechrisgrant.com

"This is my beloved son in whom I am well pleased. Listen to him"

— **God**
(Matthew 17:5)

DEDICATION

This book is dedicated to:

The late Dr. Myles Munroe
My mentor, whose work through books, CDs and seminars has inspired me to discover and pursue my life's purpose: Royalty In Paradise.

The late Alvin and Phyllis Grant
My loving parents, whose example of hard work and dedication challenge me to be persistent in life, and to pursue and fulfill my dreams.

Gabreial Alexis Grant
My precious and beloved daughter who, through her ability to receive and reciprocate love, has made fatherhood a joyful experience.

Aunt Rose
May you live long, healthy, and strong.

ACKNOWLEDGEMENTS

Creating this book has been a life-changing event. The many personal discoveries and challenges have made me more aware of the hidden treasures that lie within.

I would not have started, much less completed, this book had it not been for the relentless pursuit of my advisor, Dr. Alicia Holland-Johnson. Her support and unique leadership style have manifested what I could not initially see in myself.

I would like to thank the following friends and family members for their support. Their encouragement was the catalyst behind the completion of this book:

- Annette Grant
- Carolyn Grant
- Victor Grant
- Stacy Allen
- Marcia Lawson
- Karen Pryce

In life, you never know who is watching. Pastors Rob and Laura Koke of Shoreline Christian Center – your example of overcoming incredible odds with such grace and poise is a positive example for me to follow. Through your ministry, I have come to know, receive and embrace the unconditional love of God.

INTRODUCTION

It was in the fall of 2006 when God woke me up and asked me to start a line of clothing for Him. The conversation went something like this:

God: Wake up.
Me: Okay (but I went back to sleep).
God: Chris, wake up, I need to talk to you.
Me: Okay. What do You want to talk about?
God: I want you to start a line of clothing.
Me: But You own everything. Why do You want me to start a line of clothing?
God: Put my name on it and take it to my people.

At work a week later, I heard a voice that said, "It is time for the logo; let's take a walk." I got up from my seat and walked outside. As I exited the building, I was led to a walking trail nearby. I soon came upon a small, make-shift bridge. As I approached it, I began to cry uncontrollably. People were passing by, but no one stopped. There was no reason for me to cry, but somehow I knew it was God crying through me.

I quietly asked Him what was wrong. He replied, "This is what they do to me every day." I asked, "What do they do to You every day?" He said, "People come to me and ask if they are in good standing with me, and if I am okay with them? When I tell them yes, they say thanks, turn around and walk away."

It was at that moment when I intuitively knew what He meant. You see, the bridge (Jesus) represents our access to God the Father.

He longs for a personal loving relationship with us, but most of us are more satisfied with an assurance from God than a relationship with Him. How do you know if you are preoccupied with assurance? If all you think about and talk about is going to heaven when you die. Going to heaven should be a non-factor. If you have a personal and loving relationship with the Creator of the universe, don't you think He will gladly invite you and bring you into His kingdom?

That day, No EGO Apparel was formed and positioned as the "inspirational casual wear" brand for the believer.

THE NO EGO MESSAGE:

All people are created in the image and likeness of a loving God who passionately pursues us. To think, behave or feel any less is edging God out. Our message is simple; **No Edging God Out (EGO), Just Represent!**

THE NO EGO MISSION:

To encourage positive transformation through inspirational casual wear by reminding all people they are loved, valued and competent so they may think, behave and feel better about themselves.

THE NO EGO SLOGAN:

No EGO, Just Represent!

This book serves as an extension to the No EGO movement. It will help to communicate the truth that we do not work to earn our value; instead, we work because we are already valued. This bestowed value is called "worth." It is my sincere desire that all people who read this book will have a soul restoration and a new appreciation for themselves and others.

TABLE OF CONTENTS

Chapter One: The Mental Blueprint 13

Chapter Two: Missing the Mark 24

Chapter Three: Sin No More 36

Chapter Four: What Are You Looking At? 42

Chapter Five: Living Worthy 51

Chapter Six: The Condemnation Script 56

Chapter Seven: Be Deserving 61

Chapter Eight: Be Great 70

Chapter Nine: Success Habits of the Worthy 75

Chapter Ten: Lead Your Life 82

Chapter Eleven: A Cloud of Witness 85

Chapter Twelve: The X Factor 93

Chapter One
THE MENTAL BLUEPRINT

Prayer
Father, in the name of Jesus I come to you with a heart of gratitude, thanking you for everyone who will read this book. I pray that you will meet them at their point of need right now. Amen.

Every failure or unfulfilled dream, great or small, may be linked to a condemning thought. For as a man thinks and continues to think in his heart so is he. Every success or fulfilled desire, great or small, may be linked to a worthy thought. For as a man thinks and continues to think in his heart so is he. Our thoughts are like blueprints with which we build our lives. I call these thoughts MENTAL BLUEPRINTS.

> For we know that the things which are seen were made by things unseen.

Every thought has an associated image which, if held on to, will eventually begin to manifest itself.

Simply put, what you see is what you get. We think in pictures. Every thought is a mini movie, We call this "imagination." We can use those thoughts to entertain or drain us.

My friend, Lisa, likes to watch movies that make her cry, and I always wonder about that. Why would a person spend money, time and energy watching something that causes her to become an emotional wreck? It's not for me. Give me some comedy — I want to laugh until I fall out my seat. Give me some action — I want to conquer evil, save the world, rescue and kiss the girl.

I don't know about you, but I am well aware of the negative images that I hold in my mind daily. Because of my awareness, I can use my personal authority and power to change those negative images by choosing an empowering thought. Those who are unaware of the fact that their thoughts govern their behavior are doomed until they become aware. We call this unconscious incompetence; we don't know that we don't know.

Usain Bolt, the fastest man in the world, was favored to win the 100m sprints at the 2011 World Athletics Championships in Daegu, Japan. However, as the starter brought the athletes to the set position, Usain bolted out of his blocks with total disregard for the starting pistol. No one needed to tell him he had picked the start. Without hesitation and with total disgust, he pulled off his shirt and walked away from the starting lineup with gestures of total disbelief as he exclaimed "Too Easy!".

What was going on in the mind of the world's fastest man? How could he, after all the hard work, forfeit thousands of dollars in prize money, a sure gold medal and all the other benefits that come with winning? These are the words of the man himself: "I heard a voice in my head say go and I went."

Can you tell what was condemning about that voice? Here's the answer: you don't go until you here the gun. When you decide to do the right thing at the wrong time you get pain. To Mr. Bolt's credit, he would return three days later to win the 200m final. That's what champions are made of. They bounce back after a failure.

> **REFLECTION QUESTIONS FOR YOU**
>
> 1. What condemning thoughts do you allow yourself to think?
> 2. What worthy thoughts do you allow yourself to think?
> 3. Do the movies you script, direct, produce and watch entertain or drain you?
> 4. Are you aware of your thoughts and their impact on your behavior?
> 5. Are your thoughts causing you money, fame, glory and the fulfillment of your dreams and desires?

CAUSES THAT CONTRIBUTE TO CONDEMNING YOUR WORTHY THOUGHTS

There are several causes that may contribute to a person walking in or forfeiting the right and privilege to embrace, enjoy and experience his or her God-given destiny. In this chapter, we will examine seven such causes. They are:

ANCESTRAL	GENERATIONAL PATTERNS	ENVIRONMENTAL PRESSURES
REBELLION	MENTAL THOUGHTS	BELIEF SYSTEMS
	IGNORANCE	

Ancestral

When I speak of ancestry, I am not referring to the color of your skin or the pigment of your eyes, but rather to the origin or inception of a common thought – good or bad – that may be traced to someone within or outside of your blood line. You can't recall when you began thinking this way; all you know is that you do. It is like you were born this way. As far as you can remember, you have been using phrases such as "that's what we think" and "that's what we believe."

Here are a few examples:

- Certain races are superior.
- Certain genders are inferior.
- Certain career choices are beneath us.
- Certain career choices are for men or women only.
- We do not inter marry certain races.
- Nothing good comes from this bloodline or community.

REFLECTION QUESTIONS FOR YOU

1. Have you ever wondered who in your ancestry started these patterns of thoughts that you seem to embrace as a part of your legacy?
2. What ancestral thoughts do you hold to be true?
3. Do these thoughts empower or disempower you? Why or why not?

Generational Patterns

A generation is defined as people living around the same time and having similar ideas, problems or attitudes. Therefore, a generational pattern seems inevitable. The focus is not the generation, but the pattern. An example of a generational pattern would be an entire family line – including grandparents, parents, children and grandchildren – deciding to be doctors, lawyers or entrepreneurs.

On the other hand, you could have a generation of people who decide they would like to be welfare recipients or criminals. The purpose of this book is not to judge, but rather to act as a catalyst in starting public and private conversations and discussions about what worthy or condemning thoughts were behind these decisions. There are numerous generational patterns of which I am confident you could make your own list. Here are examples of others:

A generation of football, baseball or basketball players
A generation of teenage pregnancy
A generation of alcoholic and drug addicts
A generation of preachers

Make a list of generational patterns that exist in your family.
1.
2.
3.

Identify and explain which patterns empower or disempower you.
1.
2.
3.

Environmental Pressures

"Show me your company and I can tell you who you are."

This is the phrase that comes to mind when I think of environmental pressures. We all may recall instances when we felt pressured by others to think, behave or feel a certain way. For me, it was the pressure of becoming sexually active as a teenager. As a track and field athlete, there were no lack of opportunities from the girls who wanted to be near us so-called jocks, coupled and reinforced by the daily locker room sex talks. I recall one day being pressured to tell of my sexual exploits. The conversation went something like this.

Teammate: Why are you always so quiet when we talk about sex?
Are you a virgin or something?

Me: I am no virgin! I just like to listen to you guys talk; gentlemen don't tell.
From what I hear, you guys are amateurs.

Teammates: Amateurs? Well tell us what you do and with whom you do it, bad ass.

Me: Alright.

I told them all I did and with whom. I even included names of girls they would all fantasize about. That rendition earned me the nickname "CASANOVA." Little did they know it was all my imagination.

On the other hand, I have had many positive experiences with environmental pressures. One of those experiences was training with Olympians in Houston, Texas. Their commitment, dedication and sacrifice to their sports caused me to raise my game in many areas of my life. Because of that experience, I now know what is possible for me – assuming I am willing to focus on what I want, decide what I am willing to give in exchange for it, make a plan and work that plan.

Other environmental pressures that inspire me are men and women like you who are committed to family, a life of faith, integrity, honor, decency and the betterment of humanity.

REFLECTION QUESTIONS FOR YOU

1. What environmental pressures do you experience daily?
2. Do they empower or disempower you? Why or why not?

Rebellion

The word rebellion is normally used in a negative light, and rightfully so. But it can also be used in a positive light. Here are two examples to demonstrate how being rebellious may be used for good and bad.

Rebellion for Good

To be in rebellion means to resist or defy any control, authority or tradition. One such defiance took place in December 1955 during a typical evening rush hour in Montgomery, Alabama. A 42-year-old woman took a seat on a bus on her way home from the Montgomery Fair Department store where she worked as a seamstress. Before she reached her destination, she quietly set off a social revolution when the bus driver instructed her to move to the back of the bus. But she refused. Ms. Rosa Parks, an African American, was arrested that day for violating a city law requiring racial segregation on public buses. Her quiet act of defiance resonated throughout the world. Ms. Rosa Parks is known and revered as the "Mother of the Civil Rights Movement."

Rebellion for Bad

As I travel the world, I see a lot of evidence of negative rebellion. This type of rebellion originates from selfishness, bitterness and resentment. For instance, scripture teaches us that Adam and Eve's lives changed drastically because they decided to defy their creator and eat the forbidden fruit. Many teenage drug and alcohol abusers, along with teens who become pregnant, are not products of parental neglect. Rather, it is their defiance toward moral parental guidelines. My heart aches as I remember a time in my own life when I wanted my own way. I had wonderful parents who loved me. Casting aside all parental wisdom, teachings and experience, like the prodigal son, I ran with the wrong crowd by lying, cheating and stealing. But one day I came to my senses. If you are in defiance of what you know to be good, right and true, then for God's sake, your sake and the sake of your loved ones, stop rebelling. Receive love from God, yourself and your family.

REFLECTION QUESTIONS FOR YOU
1. Do you remember a time when you were in rebellion? Why or why not?
2. What condemning or worthy thoughts triggered your behavior?
3. Did rebelling empower or disempower you?

Mental Thoughts

You've heard it said: the mind is a terrible thing to waste. Why is this so? It is because our mental state determines our quality of life? As scripture put's it: *"As a man repeatedly thinks in his heart so is he."*

Have you ever had the experience of a thought entering your mind and for the whole day you either felt great pleasure or tremendous pain? This happens because you went for a ride on the train of thought. A train of thought is a succession of connected ideas which create a path of reasoning normally in an orderly sequence. Some people have taken the train of thought to Pity Parties, Lonesomeville, Regretful Island and Lovers Leap, just to name a few. Our ability to choose our thoughts is most vitally important to our state of being. There are volumes of books written about this topic. The most concise advice on thought control is found in Philippians 4:8 *"Whatsoever things are true, whatsoever things are honest, whatsoever things are just, whatsoever things are pure, whatsoever things are lovely whatsoever things are of a good report, if there be any virtue if there be any praise, think on these things."*

REFLECTION QUESTIONS FOR YOU
1. Where does your train of thoughts take you?
2. Do you know you can change trains if you do not like where you are heading?
3. Does your train of thought empower or disempower you? Why or why not?

Belief Systems

According to Dr Joseph Murphy in his book titled "The Power of Your Subconscious Mind," the law of the mind is the law of belief. This means to believe in the way our mind works; to believe in belief itself. The belief of our minds is the thoughts of our minds. That's it —just that and nothing else. You can tell what you believe by what you are thinking.

All of our experiences, events, conditions and acts are the reactions of our subconscious minds to our thoughts. Dr. Murphy went on to say that it is not the thing believed in, but the belief in our own minds, which brings about the result.

Whosoever, shall say to this mountain, be removed and be cast into the sea and shall not doubt in his heart but shall believe that those things which he say and continue to say shall come to pass, he shall have whatsoever he say and continue to say.

You may believe in God, but don't believe he is your healer. So instead of confessing that you are the healed of the Lord, you will tell anyone who will listen how bad you feel and how much it hurts.

You may believe in God, but don't believe he is your provider. So instead of reminding yourself that he is Jehovah Jira, you will spend the time worrying about how you are going to get your needs met. You have what you say and what you say is what you believe. Don't be fooled…you do not have to speak verbally to say something. *And she said within herself, "if I could but touch the hem of his garment I will be made whole."*

Cease believing in false beliefs, superstitions and man-made fears. Start believing in the eternal truth of your life which never changes. Jesus said, "*I am come that you may have life and life more abundantly.*" Did Jesus come? Did he deliver? Then it is time for you to start reconditioning your mind to always think with abundance. A mindset lacking abundance is false believing. An abundance mindset is right believing. Do not forget the law of your mind: what you think about you bring about.

> **REFLECTION QUESTIONS FOR YOU**
>
> 1. What do you say and continue to say?
> 2. What do you believe and continue to believe?
> 3. Does your belief system empower or disempower you? Why or why not?

Ignorance

Ignorance is not bliss. What you don't know could be hurting you right now.

My people are destroyed because of a lack of knowledge; they are destroyed because they have rejected knowledge.

How many times have you used the phrase "I don't want to know?"

The lack of information about anything will almost always contribute to poor decision making.

> **REFLECTION QUESTIONS FOR YOU**
>
> 1. Knowing what you know now, would you still marry the person you married?
> 2. Knowing what you know now, would you still choose the same career?
> 3. Knowing what you know now, would you still start or buy the business you started or bought?
> 4. Did not knowing empower or disempower you? Why or why not?

While ignorance may cause poor judgment, here are some occasions in which I enjoy being ignorant:

A surprise birthday party
A surprise bonus, raise or promotion
A surprise gift
A surprise discount

What surprises do you like?
What surprises don't you like?

Here is the truth about being ignorant: you can choose to be in the know. If not knowing can drastically alter your life negatively, then you owe it to yourself to receive knowledge. People who think they are worthy seek out knowledge.

I said earlier that what you think about you bring about.

REFLECTION QUESTIONS FOR YOU

1. Did you know that?
2. If you did not know, how did not knowing affect you then?
3. How will knowing affect you now?

Chapter Two
MISSING THE MARK

> ### Prayer
> Lord, we thank you that we are secure in you because we know that when we miss the mark your goodness and mercy is ours for the asking in Jesus' name. Amen

Pete and Patricia are the model couple in their neighborhood. Their deep sense of care, affection and love for each other can hardly go unnoticed. Patricia enjoys spending time with Pete and often discusses plans of building their dream home. Pete, wanting to please the love of his life, works overtime every chance he has. Patricia wants her dream home, but is beginning to miss spending quality time with Pete. Soon there is resentment, and they begin to drift apart. As Pete dragged home late from work one day, she met him at the door fuming like a pit bull.

Patricia: We never spend time together anymore! You are always gone!

Pete: What do you want me to do? I am doing this for you. I am tired and don't want to hear any bullsh*t!

The next day, feeling unmotivated and not knowing what to do, Pete reached out to Pam, his coworker, to get another woman's perspective on his situation.

Pam: She is tripping; she does not know the price of her dream or whom she's got for that matter. I would not do that to you if I were in her shoes.

As they talked, time went by unnoticed.

Pete: You are so easy to talk to. Thanks for taking the time.
I appreciate it. I'll see you tomorrow.
Pam: Here is my number. Call me if you want to talk.

Pete pondered the conversation he had with Pam as he drove home. "She does not know the price of her dream. Lord, tell me what to say so Patricia may understand," he murmured to himself. Pete stopped at the local flower shop and bought a half-dozen roses for his wife as a makeup strategy. "I will give her one rose first to let her know how special she is to me, and then the other five as I ask for her forgiveness," he said to himself.

With the flowers behind his back, he knocked on the front door. Patricia walked to the door and opened it, then took two steps back, folded her arms and looked at him with eyes that cut through him like a knife.

Patricia: Where were you? You were supposed to be home three hours ago. Are you cheating on me?

Pete dared not tell her he was with another woman discussing their business.

Pete: Sorry, I was out with the fellas, I just lost track of time.
Patricia: Don't lie to me! Paul came by looking for you.
Pete: You are tripping! Do you know how many women would love to be in your position having a man like me?
Patricia: Women? What women? Get the F out of here you lying MF!

Pete threw the flowers at her feet, stormed out of the house, got in his car and sped out of the driveway. He picked up his cell phone and dialed the number Pam gave him.

Pam: Hello, who is this?
Pete: It's me, Pete.
Pam: I did not expect to hear from you so soon.
Pete: I know; you were right, she is tripping. Can we talk in person?
Pam: Sure, I was heading to the shower when you called. My address is 2222 Backlash Road. I'll see you when you get here.

Pam hurried to the bathroom, forgetting her clothes and towel on her bed. Minutes later she heard the doorbell ring.

Pam: Who is it?
Pete: It's me
Pam: Come in, I will be with you shortly.

As Pam stepped out of the shower she realized she had left her towel and clothes on her bed. Without thinking, she decided to make a run to her bedroom without Pete seeing her nakedness. As she opened the bathroom door, there stood Pete steering directly at her. Instinctively, he moved toward her, kissed her and she responded in kind. They found themselves all over each other. Pete's mental frustration had collided with Pam's pent up sexual frustration. As they held each other, there were no need for words as their bodies did all the talking…

The story of Pete and Patricia is an example of what goes on in people's lives every day. It is meant to illustrate how sin is the result of poor judgment. Poor judgment, if you recall, may be attributed to the rejection or the lack of knowledge which is linked to an unworthy thought.

Food for thought

Sin is not a person, but an event.

WHAT IS SIN?

The word sin is an archery term, which means to miss the mark or bulls eye. No archer in his right mind aims and shoots with the intention of missing the bull's eye. Even if he should miss the mark a thousand times, he is not called sinner. A lousy archer, maybe. But not sinner. In spiritual terms, sin is missing the mark of God's standard of what is right for our lives. Or you may say what's right for himself (we are his image). In the previous story, we see evidence of sin in lying and adultery. While this may be obvious, have you ever wondered what is the root cause? You guessed it: condemnation. We will deal with this in detail a bit later.

Lying and adultery are mere symptoms or fruits. The real issue is what's at the root. God is not concerned with your fruits of sin. He is concerned with your root of condemnation. They say a city inspector will not condemn a building for issues above the foundation. However, if the foundation is faulty, it must be condemned. Like the city inspector, this book was written to help you identify and condemn your condemning thoughts. A mindset of condemnation is unfit to live in. This book will help you move out and locate to a more solid foundation, one that is condemnation free and one that has been built, tested, inspected and approved.

Here is a perfect illustration of sin. If you drive a car that requires gasoline and you put water in the gas tank, would you expect it to function properly? No. The manufacturer designed, developed and tested the proper function of the vehicle using gasoline. In a similar way, you and I were created to function in a certain way with ourselves and with each other. When we operate out of character, we are malfunctioning (sinning).

Genesis 1 tells us that we are created in God's image and have been crowned with glory and honor. There is no glory in adultery. Where is the honor in lying? We essentially dumb down when we sin. We violate ourselves by choosing condemning thoughts to guide our decisions. These thoughts may be driven by fear of rejection or fear of consequences. At any rate, we devalue ourselves by falling short of

God's glorious design of a person who thinks enough of himself to always tell the truth. It's about integrity. Who I am, what I say and what I do are the same. As the saying goes, "there is no shame in my game."

Adultery is much deeper than having sex with a person who is not your spouse. Let's broaden the scope by looking at a statement found in scripture:

> *A wicked and adulterous generation asks for a sign.*
> — Matthew 16:4

"What's wicked and adulterous about asking for a sign?" you may ask. "I should be allowed to believe it when I see it; that's fear to me" you may argue. Not so. To ask for a sign before you believe is a violation of the law of belief. You must first believe it, and then you will see it. Asking for a sign is also a statement of doubt in the ability of the Creator to do what He promised. Without faith, it is impossible to please Him. Adultery, then, is to make a faith covenant that certain needs will be met in a certain way, and then breaking that agreement.

We do not ask the ground to give us a harvest before we plant a seed; that is considered agricultural adultery. The promise is: *while the earth remains, there will be seed, time and harvest.* I can hear someone arguing with the earth right now.

> **You:** Hey earth, I am starving. Could you give me a harvest?
> **Earth:** You know the rules. Give me a seed and, in time, I will give you the harvest.
> **You:** How are you going to do that?
> **Earth:** None of your business; just give me the damn seed!
> **You:** How do I know this is not a scam?
> **Earth:** You wicked, adulterous unbeliever!

Here are a few statements to ponder:

If you believe it is God's will for you to be healthy, then sickness is a sin.

If you believe it is God's will for you to live in abundance, then poverty is a sin.

THE POWER OF SIN

I like sports, especially the game of football. The objective is to score while preventing the other team from scoring. The great teams are all about intimidation. Their agenda is to get the opposing team to feel small and hopeless in their presence. In a similar way, the power of sin lies in its ability to get you to see how badly you have messed up instead of how wonderful and amazing you are. The strength of sin is the law. Have you ever found yourself driving somewhere, and instead of enjoying the ride and focusing on the road, you spend all your time looking for the cops? Why do we do that? We do it because we are more conscious of being pulled over by them for a violation. Simply put, we are sin conscious. Sin intimidates.

THE PURPOSE OF SIN

The purpose of sin is to get your attention. It wants you to be preoccupied with looking at it instead of your dreams and goals. As long as you keep thinking about how badly you blew it, sin is empowered. Feelings of frustration and hopelessness are clues that sin is having its way; you are not getting the results you want.

Weight loss has been a hot button topic for many years. I have had conversations with men and women who tell me that they want to lose weight because they are fat. If you are one of those people, then you are playing right into the hands of sin. You must have a clear image of what you want to look like, then think, say and act like you are already that way. Here is the secret for those of you who want to lose weight: don't try to lose weight. That's right. Rather, see yourself fit and trim (identity). *Be not conformed to the pattern of this world but be transformed by the renewing of your mind.* Your ability to see yourself that way will inspire you to change behavior. You can see an image of fit and trim, but not an image of losing weight. Say and be what you are.

I know you may be thinking: Is being fat a sin? The answer is yes if your goal, dream and intention is to be fit and trim. To him who knows the truth and doeth it not to him it is sin. What is the truth about you? You are not your body. You are spirit who lives in a body and, as such, possess the personal power and authority to change house when you feel like it. Remember, you are only fat because of ignorance. What you think about, you bring about. I can assure you there are thousands of fit and trim people right now who were most likely in your shoes. The reason you are still fat is because you do not see yourself worthy of being fit and trim. See yourself fit and trim; you are worthy.

THE PARDON OF SIN

The Emancipation Proclamation
January 1, 1863

By the President of the United States of America:
A Proclamation.

Whereas, on the twenty-second day of September, in the year of our Lord one thousand eight hundred and sixty-two, a proclamation was issued by the President of the United States, containing, among other things, the following, to wit:

"That on the first day of January, in the year of our Lord one thousand eight hundred and sixty-three, all persons held as slaves within any State or designated part of a State, the people whereof shall then be in rebellion against the United States, shall be then, thenceforward, and forever free; and the Executive Government of the United States, including the military and naval authority thereof, will recognize and maintain the freedom of such persons, and will do no act or acts to repress such persons, or any of them, in any efforts they may make for their actual freedom.

...

And by virtue of the power, and for the purpose aforesaid, I do order and declare that all persons held as slaves within said designated States, and parts of States, are, and henceforward shall be free; and that the Executive government of the United States, including the military and naval authorities thereof, will recognize and maintain the freedom of said persons.

And I hereby enjoin upon the people so declared to be free to abstain from all violence, unless in necessary self-defense; and I recommend to them that, in all cases when allowed, they labor faithfully for reasonable wages.

And I further declare and make known, that such persons of suitable condition, will be received into the armed service of the United States to garrison forts, positions, stations, and other places, and to man vessels of all sorts in said service.

And upon this act, sincerely believed to be an act of justice, warranted by the Constitution, upon military necessity, I invoke the considerate judgment of mankind, and the gracious favor of Almighty God.

In witness whereof, I have hereunto set my hand and caused the seal of the United States to be affixed.

Done at the City of Washington, this first day of January, in the year of our Lord one thousand eight hundred and sixty three, and of the Independence of the United States of America the eighty-seventh.

By the President: ABRAHAM LINCOLN
WILLIAM H. SEWARD, Secretary of State

The Emancipation Proclamation was signed into law by President Abraham Lincoln in 1863. It declared, among other things, that all slaves in any state that is in rebellion against the United States were henceforth and forever free, and that such freedom will be recognized and maintained by the U.S. government using military and naval force if necessary.

What a day this must have been for every man, woman and child held as slaves in these states. What joy and jubilation this must have been for them when word came of their freedom. I can see them dancing. I can hear them singing and shouting, "I am free! You are free! We are free!"

I can also see the sad and disgusted faces of all the slave masters as they exclaim, "What are we going to do about our cattle, tobacco and cotton? Who is going to work in the fields now?"

With the stroke of a pen, life for slaves and slave masters were changed forever. Slavery was now illegal. In the document, President Lincoln went on to say that he believed his action was an act of justice warranted by the Constitution. The implications of such a statement are too many to discuss in this book. However, here are a few questions to ponder:

What did those men, women and precious children do to deserve being transported from Africa and sold into slavery?

What did the children and grandchildren born to these slaves do to warrant them being slaves?

If you are still pondering, here is the answer: they did nothing. They were sold and born into a lifestyle of slavery. Can you hear justice as she screams at the top of her lungs, "Set them free!" Even though justice cried, it did not set them free. It was something more powerful – grace.

What did the slaves do to earn their freedom? Nothing! According to the emancipation document, it was the sole will of President Lincoln to set them free. No court, no judge, no jury. Just an executive decision.

In a similar way, over 2000 years ago, God made an executive decision to redeem mankind by sending his son, Jesus Christ, to the cross to die and pay the penalty for all of humanity's sin. His action signified that every man, woman and child tricked or born into sin (slavery) was henceforth and forever free. Sins past, present and future were no longer to be assessed against humanity. Simply put, sin was abolished and righteousness was the order of the day. Like my son puts it, "Sin is wack, and righteousness is the new swagger forever!"

Here are excerpts from God's Emancipation Proclamation Declaration.

> For God so loved the world that he gave his one and only Son, that whoever believes in him shall not perish but have eternal life. For God did not send his Son into the world to condemn the world, but to save the world through him. —JOHN 3:16-17

> You see, at just the right time, when we were still powerless, Christ died for the ungodly. Very rarely will anyone die for a righteous person, though for a good person someone might possibly dare to die. But God demonstrates his own love for us in this: While we were still sinners, Christ died for us. Since we have now been justified by his blood, how much more shall we be saved from God's wrath through him! For if, while we were God's enemies, we were reconciled to him through the death of his Son, how much more, having been reconciled, shall we be saved through his life! Not only is this so, but we also boast in God through our Lord Jesus Christ, through whom we have now received reconciliation. —ROMANS 5

DEATH THROUGH ADAM, LIFE THROUGH CHRIST

> Therefore, just as sin entered the world through one man, and death through sin, and in this way death came to all people, because all sinned—To be sure, sin was in the world before the law was given, but sin is not charged against anyone's account where there is no law. Nevertheless, death reigned from the time of Adam to the time of Moses, even over those who did not sin by breaking a command, as did Adam, who is a pattern of the one to come.

> But the gift is not like the trespass. For if the many died by the trespass of the one man, how much more did God's grace and the gift that

came by the grace of the one man, Jesus Christ, overflow to the many! Nor can the gift of God be compared with the result of one man's sin: The judgment followed one sin and brought condemnation, but the gift followed many trespasses and brought justification. For if, by the trespass of the one man, death reigned through that one man, how much more will those who receive God's abundant provision of grace and of the gift of righteousness reign in life through the one man, Jesus Christ! Consequently, just as one trespass resulted in condemnation for all people, so also one righteous act resulted in justification and life for all people. For just as through the disobedience of the one man the many were made sinners, so also through the obedience of the one man the many will be made righteous.

The law was brought in so that the trespass might increase. But where sin increased, grace increased all the more, so that, just as sin reigned in death, so also grace might reign through righteousness to bring eternal life through Jesus Christ our Lord. So that, [just] as sin has reigned in death, [so] grace (His unearned favor) might reign also through righteousness (right standing with God) which issues in eternal life through Jesus Christ (the Messiah, the Anointed One) our Lord. —ROMANS 5

The God of the universe is not counting sin against us any longer. He only cares about our righteousness. This free gift of righteousness will be recognized and maintained by God himself. That means it is foolish to worry about your right standing with God. We are righteous. That's it, period. End of story. Accept it.

I can hear someone saying "But…" Sit you butt down. You had no say in being declared a sinner, and you had no say in being declared righteous. Your attitude should be one of gratitude. I am righteous, you are righteous, we are righteous. That's right, that's good news.

Oh, I feel like running and leaping and shouting and praising God right now. It's time for a praise break! Alleluia! Alleluia! Alleluia!

Okay, I am back.

If you can identify with this truth, then would you please help me tell every man, woman and child that the power of sin is broken over their lives and that they are right with God? Tell the prostitutes (male and female) they don't have to do that anymore. Tell the drug addicts they don't have to do that anymore. Tell the self-righteous they don't have to pretend any longer, that their self-effort is unacceptable. Whatever your race, nationality, gender, religious affiliation, social status or economic status, you are made right by God through His son, Jesus Christ. Believe, receive, embrace and share.

Chapter Three
SIN NO MORE

Prayer
Lord, we thank you for a life of victory that we have in you through your son, our brother, Jesus Christ. Amen.

In the previous chapter, we came to understand what sin is and how it has been dealt with at the cross by our heavenly father through our elder brother, Jesus. In this chapter, we will unveil the secret to Jesus living a sinless life and how we may walk in his footsteps, if we so choose.

> **The Principle of Condemnation**
>
> We sin because we condemn ourselves. Condemnation is the root cause for sin.

UNVEILING THE REASON WE MISS THE MARK

In John Chapter 8, the story goes:

Jesus went unto the Mount of Olives. And early in the morning he came again into the temple, and all the people came unto him; and he sat down, and taught them. And the scribes and Pharisees brought unto him a woman taken in adultery; and when they had set her in the midst, they say unto him, Master, this woman was taken in adultery, in the very act. Now Moses in the law commanded us, that such should be stoned: but what sayest thou?

This they said, tempting him that they might have to accuse him. But Jesus stooped down, and with his finger wrote on the ground, as though he heard them not.

So when they continued asking him, he lifted up himself, and said unto them, He that is without sin among you, let him first cast a stone at her. And again he stooped down, and wrote on the ground.

And they which heard it, being convicted by their own conscience, went out one by one, beginning at the eldest, even unto the last: and Jesus was left alone, and the woman standing in the midst.

When Jesus had lifted up himself, and saw none but the woman, he said unto her, Woman, where are those thine accusers? Hath no man condemned thee? She said, No man, Lord. And Jesus said unto her, neither do I condemn you: go, and sin no more.

Then spake Jesus again unto them, saying, I am the light of the world: he that followeth me shall not walk in darkness, but shall have the light of life.

> Jesus said **"I am the light of the world: he that follows me shall not walk in darkness, but shall have the light of life."**

THE LIGHT IS ON

John clearly told us that Jesus' intention was to get to the temple early so He could teach the people. He was on a mission, and He was passionate and focused. Therefore, the interruption by the scribes and Pharisees must be perceived as a divine object lesson. The story tells us that they brought the woman caught in adultery in the very act. She was getting her freak on with no regards to consequences.

Have you ever been caught freaking?
　Freaking liar
　Freaking thief
　Freaking murderer
　Freaking backbiter
　Freaking gossiper

They threw her in the middle. This means the spotlight was no longer on Jesus, but on the woman. That is what the devil wants to do to you. He wants to put you on blast. He wants to shame you. He knows that if he can get to you, then he can get to the Jesus in you. You will begin to doubt the greater power within. You may find yourself saying things like:

Am I really saved? If I am saved, then why do I keep doing the same thing over and over knowing that it is wrong? Does He have the power to protect me from all of this?

I need to pray more, fast more, read the Bible more, worship God more, love more, go to church more. I feel so helpless. Darn, I need a drink. I know what I will do – I will sell everything, give the money to charity and move away from all of this distraction.

Did you say money? Give me the money; then you may move away.

Just kidding. I am here and Jesus is here. That means the light is on!

John told us the enemy was after Jesus. He was just using the woman to get to Him. He knows who we are. As such, we must do like Jesus did: ignore, stoop and write. Ignore the accusation the enemy hurls at you, stoop in submission to God signifying that He is your father and the Lord of your life, and then write. Writing is a manual way of printing or expressing what is written on our hearts.

　Write: I am the righteousness of God in Christ Jesus.
　Write: My name is written in the lamb's book of life.
　Write: Greater is he that is within me, than he that is in the world.
　Write: Jesus paid it all.
　Write: I am accepted in the beloved.

This is called building up yourself in the most holy faith. It is encouraging yourself in the Lord.

Do you get it? Stay close, we are half way there.

John told us the accusers would not quit while Jesus ignored, stooped and wrote. They kept bombarding him with the same question: "The law says stone her, but what do you say?"

The writer says that Jesus stood up and said to them, "He that is without sin among you, let him first cast a stone at her."

Now that is how you silence the accuser. What's good for the goose is good for the gander. You want to throw stones, then prepare to be stoned. What a shift of events. The spotlight was now on them. Is it getting clearer now? There is no way your accusers can call you out without being called out themselves. In order to show you up, they have to step into the light.

Be like Jesus. Rise up, take authority and declare:

I am forgiven, are you?

I am heaven bound, are you?

I received Jesus as my savior, did you?

Now, stoop and write:

I thank you LORD for saving me. Thank you for restoring me. Thank you! Thank you! Thank you!

Are your accusers still around? Look…see them walking away, see them running away, see them scatter. The enemy may come at you one way, but will have to flea seven ways. Yeah, yeah! Get out of here! Run you coward! Run! Hahahaha! This is how we do it.

Now it should be just you, me and Jesus. You did well. But we are not done yet. It is now time to unveil the secret behind why we sin, and time to stop the harassments once and for all. John wrote, when Jesus had lifted himself up and saw nobody but the woman. He said "Woman, where are your accusers? Did any of them condemn you? She said, "No man, Lord." And Jesus said unto her, "Neither do I condemn you. Go and sin (do not condemn yourself) no more."

Do you understand?

In the judicial system, convicted criminals are not allowed to be a part of the jury pool and are not considered a credible witness. That is what happened to the accusers. They were all convicted and, as such, were not allowed to condemn anyone. Jesus, the perfect juror, said "Neither do I condemn you." (for God did not send his son into the world to condemn the world but that the world through him might be saved). It is not in Jesus' best interest to condemn. As a matter of fact, it would be a breach of his delegated authority, an abuse of power.

The accusers could not condemn her, and Jesus did not condemn her. Therefore, the only person left was the woman. Jesus advice was for her to go and not condemn herself any more.

Do you get it? Jesus' object lesson was, "Behind every sin is a condemning thought." Let's test and prove.

Question: Why do people lie?
Answer: Because they believe they will be rejected or punished for telling the truth.

Question: Why do people steal?
Answer: Fear of rejection.

Question: Why did Adam and Eve disobey God?
Answer: They did not see themselves as gods. They thought they were missing out.

Question: Why do people go after other gods?
Answer: They don't believe the true God is trustworthy, or is able to meet their needs.

Conduct your own experiment. Sin is scientific, as is righteousness. Take a minute and let it soak in. Remember: light's on. Now you know the truth about why we sin, and why Jesus did not. If you decide to practice sinning after this revelation, then you do so because you want to. No sweat – this is the dispensation of grace. God was in Christ reconciling the world to himself, not counting man's sin against him. God's not counting; only the people with whom you interact daily are.

Honestly, from an athlete perspective, sin is no fun because the one who matters is not keeping score. It is like shooting a basketball and scoring while out of bounds or, better yet, when the shot clock is off. Sin is out of bounds for the believer. Stay within the bounds of righteousness and keep shooting. We do not shoot for victory, but from victory. We've already won. The only shot that matters was the one made by Jesus some 2000 years ago. Go and sin no more.

Chapter Four
WHAT ARE YOU LOOKING AT?

Prayer
"Thank you Father, that we have an advocate, the Holy Spirit, that intercedes on our behalf, who knows what to say when we do not, what to ask when we don't. Amen

When I was in the first grade, I was considered the dumbest kid in my class. This stigma followed me all the way to the fourth grade. I remember being held back at recess by my teacher to finish my work while the rest of the class would go out to play. I would hear children laughing and playing while I struggled to finish my assignment. This would make me so mad. Oftentimes I would cry with such loud sobs. To me it was mean, ugly and downright wrong. Why did I have to stay back and finish my work while the others got to play? After all, everyone deserves a break. The answer was obvious to others, but not to me.

The teacher knew my parents well and, unknown to me, was given free reign over me in their absence. My parents, siblings and teachers tried their best to help during those years, but with little success. I had bought into the lie. I had become accustomed to being called dumb. It shattered my self-esteem to what I considered beyond repair at the time. Adults can be mean, but kids know no bounds; they are ruthless. I did not see myself loved, valued or competent. I would hide in the restrooms for hours out of fear of going to class. Needless to say, those were miserable years.

One Sunday morning while at church, our Sunday school teacher told a story of Solomon, the wisest man who ever lived. She said he was a young man who inherited his father's throne after his father's death. However, Solomon did not know how to rule or govern the people, so he prayed and asked God to give him wisdom, knowledge and understanding…and God did. My teacher said, "You can ask God for whatever you want right now." That story caused me to change my focus from myself to God. I remember bowing my head and, with tears running down my face, saying to myself, "Lord, I don't care about wisdom, knowledge and understanding, I just want to learn how to read." And He heard me. Suddenly, things were easy to understand and school became fun. However, I did not recognize what had happen until I had graduated college. The truth is that I am intelligent. I was not dumb, I was just living out someone else beliefs. What you see is what you get. What you focus on is what you move toward. What you believe is how you behave.

Let's look at a story that brings out the concept of "See, Be, Manifest." This story is about Jacob and his uncle Laban. It is fascinating because it is essentially a blueprint on how to step up and live life on our own terms, or how to beat a conman at his own game. The story tells us that Laban had essentially agreed to pay Jacob spotted and speckled livestock for his labor. According to the Bible, Laban changed Jacob's wages ten times to his benefit. So Jacob decided this time around he would be paid on his terms.

Specifically, in Genesis Chapter 30, Jacob's strategy is revealed. Let's take a closer look at this excerpt to see exactly what happened:

> [37]*Jacob, however, took fresh-cut branches from poplar, almond and plane trees and made white stripes on them by peeling the bark and exposing the white inner wood of the branches.* [38]*Then he placed the peeled branches*

in all the watering troughs, so that they would be directly in front of the flocks when they came to drink. When the flocks were in heat and came to drink, ³⁹ they mated in front of the branches. And they bore young that were streaked or speckled or spotted. ⁴⁰ Jacob set apart the young of the flock by themselves, but made the rest face the streaked and dark-colored animals that belonged to Laban. Thus he made separate flocks for himself and did not put them with Laban's animals. ⁴¹ Whenever the stronger females were in heat, Jacob would place the branches in the troughs in front of the animals so they would mate near the branches, ⁴² but if the animals were weak, he would not place them there. So the weak animals went to Laban and the strong ones to Jacob. ⁴³ In this way the man grew exceedingly prosperous and came to own large flocks, and female and male servants, and camels and donkeys.

Now, let's put this into perspective. Jacob had observed that when the flocks came to the water gutter to drink and were in heat and mated, that they would produce young whose coats took on the pattern of what they were looking at.

With this type of revelation, Jacob decided to use it to his advantage. This is what worthy people do. They live life on their own terms. This means that sometimes you will have to break the rules. Note that I say the rules and not the law. You see, rules are sometimes made to your disadvantage, while laws are designed to benefit everyone. American history teaches us that at one point, blacks were considered two thirds of a person, which means it took two blacks to equal one vote. This was a deliberate rule that was made into law to benefit the powers that be. However, there is a Divine law that states all men are created equal. This levels the playing field to one man, one vote. Therefore, worthy people know that when there is a conflict between rule and law, the right thing to do is obey the law.

The Principle of See, Be, Manifest
You become what you focus on.

The universal principle of "See, Be, Manifest" affects all of us. You become what you focus on. Those who are aware of this principle use it to their advantage, while those unconscious to this reality are caught in a hypnotic trance that often leads to their demise. Imagine that you are at home on the couch or in the recliner watching your favorite show. You notice this commercial that tells you over and over again what you need. You turn the channel and then another commercial subliminally shares the same message—what they are promoting is right for you, was made for you, and you have to get it. Otherwise, you are missing out. You listen to them and go ahead and order that product or service. A few days later that product or service is in your home and you are confused. You don't even remember why you ordered this stuff. You ask yourself, "How did it get here? What did it cost me? Did I really need it?"

Don't feel bad…it happened to me, too. The truth of the matter is that we oftentimes order products or services that we do not need. But, for some strange reason, we just got to have them. This is the perfect example of how people get caught up in a situation that they are unconscious of and end up with an undesired outcome.

NEGATIVE MANIFESTATION

Have you ever felt that you were doing the right thing, but end up getting the raw end of the deal? Well, our ancestors, Adam and Eve, used the "See, Be, Manifest" principle negatively, and its outcome still affects us day. In Genesis Chapter 3, it states:

> **"And when the woman saw that the tree was good (suitable, pleasant) for food and that it was delightful to look at, and a tree to be desired in order to make one wise, she took of its fruit and ate; and she gave some also to her husband, and he ate. Then the eyes of them both were opened, and they knew that they were naked; and they sewed fig leaves together and made themselves apron like girdles."**

Adam and Eve thought they were going to be heroes, but ended up with zero. Satan took the kingdom of God right from under them. They were naked alright. I am bombarded with evidence of the negative manifestation of this principle everywhere I look, beginning with myself. I would like to title one of my episodes, "College freshman gone wild." Here's how this principle played a role in my life during my college freshman year:

> **MY EXAMPLE**
>
> *SEE: What was I looking at? A big butt and a smile.*
> *BE: Who did I think I was? The girl's brown sugar.*
> *MANIFEST: A 1.4 GPA after earning a 3.6 the previous semester.*

For my Dad, it was alcohol. This led to him living the life of an alcoholic for many years. But enough of me and my family; what where you looking at, and how did it affect you? Or what are you looking at today, and how is it affecting you?

Was it the girls that had you bumping into a pole? Is it the Jones' way of life that led to you filing for bankruptcy? Was it porn that caused an end to your marriage? Is it drugs that have you dependent? Was it the wrongs of someone you loved deeply that resulted in a broken relationship? Is it negative circumstances that caused you to give up on your dreams, resign the position, quit school or the business? Whatever your situation, know that this principle can work for you if you decide to focus on the things that serve your dreams, visions and goals.

A KING'S CONFESSION

King David is said to be the greatest king who ever lived. His exploits are played out on Broadway and movie screens. He was a man of valor and passion. In 2 Samuel 6, scripture tells us that after successfully bringing the ark of the covenant back to Jerusalem, he danced before the Lord, stripping down to his underwear. This made his wife so mad at him.

> **And David danced before the Lord with all his might; and David was girded with a linen ephod. So David and all the house of Israel brought up the ark of the Lord with shouting, and with the sound of the trumpet.**[6] **And as the ark of the Lord came into the city of David, Michal Saul's daughter, David's wife, looked through a window, and saw king David leaping and dancing before the Lord; and she despised him in her heart.**

One evening he went out on the terrace of his palace for a walk. As he strolled, his eyes came across a woman bathing. The Bible described her as beautiful and lovely to look at. He had laid eyes on an image his mind could not shake. The rest is history.

In 2 Samuel 11, it states:

> **In the spring, when kings go forth to battle, David sent Joab with his servants and all Israel, and they ravaged the Ammonites [country] and besieged Rabbah. But David remained in Jerusalem.**
>
> **One evening David arose from his couch and was walking on the roof of the king's house, when from there he saw a woman bathing; and she was very lovely to behold. David sent and inquired about the woman. One said, Is not this Bathsheba, the daughter of Eliam and the wife of Uriah the Hittite? And David sent messengers and took her. And she came in to him, and he lay with her—for she was purified from her uncleanness. Then she returned to her house. And the woman became pregnant and sent and told David, I am with child ...**

His story to me is an example of what can happen when valor and passion go unchecked.

Let's take this situation and apply the "See, Be, Manifest" principle:

> **THE KING'S MANIFESTATION**
>
> **SEE:** What was the king looking at? A beautiful woman taking a bath.
> **BE:** Who did he think he was? He knew he was king and could have whatever he wanted. After all, he owned her.
> **MANIFEST:** What were the manifestations? Adultery, lies, murder and cover up.

Now, read the rest of the story at your own leisure so that you can discover that King David was confronted by the Prophet Nathan. At the end of their conversation, you will notice that King David was in deep remorse. He had manifested something he did not want to associate himself with. As such, he cried out:

[1]Have mercy upon me, O God, according to your steadfast love; according to the multitude of your tender mercy *and* loving-kindness blot out my transgressions. Wash me thoroughly [and repeatedly] from my iniquity *and* guilt and cleanse me *and* make me wholly pure from my sin! For I am conscious of my transgressions *and* I acknowledge them; my sin is ever before me. Against You, You only, have I sinned and done that which is evil in your sight, so that you are justified in your sentence and faultless in your judgment. Behold, I was brought forth in [a state of] iniquity; my mother was sinful who conceived me [and I too am sinful]. Behold, you desire truth in the inner being; make me therefore to know wisdom in my inmost heart. Purify me with hyssop, and I shall be clean [ceremonially]; wash me, and I shall [in reality] be whiter than snow. Make me to hear joy and gladness *and* be satisfied; let the bones which you have broken rejoice. Hide your face from my sins and blot out all my guilt *and* iniquities. Create in me a clean heart, O God, and renew a right, persevering, *and* steadfast spirit within me. Cast me not away from your presence and take not Your Holy Spirit from me. Restore to me

the joy of your salvation and uphold me with a willing spirit. Then will I teach transgressors your ways, and sinners shall be converted *and* return to you. Deliver me from blood guiltiness *and* death, O God, the God of my salvation, *and* my tongue shall sing aloud of your righteousness (Your rightness and your justice).O Lord, open my lips, and my mouth shall show forth Your praise. For you delight not in sacrifice, or else would I give it; you find no pleasure in burnt offering. My sacrifice [the sacrifice acceptable] to God is a broken spirit; a broken and a contrite heart [broken down with sorrow for sin and humbly and thoroughly penitent], such, O God, You will not despise. Do good in your good pleasure to Zion; rebuild the walls of Jerusalem. Then will you delight in the sacrifices of righteousness, justice, *and* right, with burnt offering and whole burnt offering; then bullocks will be offered upon your altar.

And then King David goes on to commit himself to a life of integrity. In Psalms 101, David says:

" **I will behave myself wisely *and* give heed to the blameless way—O when will You come to me? I will walk within my house in integrity *and* with a blameless heart. I will set no base or wicked thing before my eyes. I hate the work of them who turn aside [from the right path]; it shall not grasp hold of me. A perverse heart shall depart from me; I will know no evil person *or* thing".**

He took responsibility for his actions and made the decision to turn his life around. That is what worthy people do. That is what kings do**.** You and I are kings. I am not talking to your flesh, but to your spirit. So whether you are male or female reading this book, it does not matter. God is spirit, God is king. We are his image.

POSITIVE MANIFESTATION

Now, let's turn our attention to see how the "See, Be, Manifest" principle can be used to manifest the good we so desire in our lives.

In Joshua 1:8, it says, **"This Book of the Law shall not depart out of your mouth, but you shall meditate on it day and night, that you may observe and do according to all that is written in it. For then you shall make your way prosperous, and then you shall deal wisely and have good success."**

The advice God gave to the man who is responsible for leading a nation into the promise land is to meditate in his laws day and night, then observe and do according to what is written. Meditation involves, at a minimum, seeing, saying and contemplating. God's promise to us is that His word, His blueprint – when followed – will cause us to have good success, the kind in which you are wealthy and healthy, famous with a fabulous family, comfortable and complete in Him. It will not be "bad success," the kind in which you have all the money, but are sick and tired all the time; all the fame, but you lose your family; or all the applause, but you are scared, lonely and unfulfilled.

Earlier, we learned how Jacob decided to live life on his terms. With the Lord as his guide, Jacob used the principle of "See, Be, Manifest," which resulted in him becoming extremely wealthy. He owned large flocks, had male and female servants and had the best rides (camels and donkeys) available all the time. Jesus said, "I am the vine, you are the branches: He that continues to abide in me, and I in him, the same will continue to bring forth much fruit, for without me you can do nothing. Herein is my Father glorified, that you bear much fruit; so shall you be my disciples."

What are you looking at? It better be the laws of your creator. He guarantees prosperity and good success.

Chapter Five
LIVING WORTHY

Prayer
Heavenly Father, I thank you for the demonstrative reminder through Jesus Christ that I am worthy of you and all the abundance you bring into my life each day. Amen.

Worthy is the lamb that was slain, and worthy are they for whom he was slain. If condemnation is the root cause for sin then how should the righteous live?

The answer is simple: live worthy.

Do you believe you were created to live a life of purpose? If the answer is yes, then a life of purpose must be lived on purpose. Don't just talk about it; embody it and be about it. Take time to evaluate and allocate the resources in your life, including your time, talent, treasure and relationships.

Time

They say time is a terrible thing to waste, and rightfully so, because it is the currency we must trade for our goals and dreams. How much time do you spend each day with matters related to the dreams and visions you have for your life? The answer you give is in direct correlation to how worthy you think you are of them.

Talent

Most people do not take the time to evaluate what they are good at, and so life for them is "outer worldly." By that, I mean they are always looking for something outside of themselves to make them happy or fulfilled. Here is the truth about humans: we were created to dominate in an area of gifting, therefore there is no fulfillment until we first discover, develop and deliver our talents to the world. Jesus said it best: "I did not come to be served but to serve and to give my life a ransom for many." So, take the time to discover, develop and deliver your talent to the world. You are worthy, and the world is worthy of you.

Treasure

Those who believe in the beauty of their dreams have no trouble spending the necessary time, energy and resources in pursuit of them. What do you treasure? Will it matter six months from now? Will it leave a lasting legacy? People who know they are worthy take the time to prioritize what they treasure and ensure their decisions are in alignment with the dreams and vision they have for their lives.

THE WORTHY LIFE

The worthy life is a distinguished life of significance, lived to please one while serving many. All of us were created with something special that the world needs. We call this a gift. A gift is never for itself, but rather is carefully selected by the giver and is delivered to the receiver in hopes of serving him or her. The gift then conveys to the receiver that he or she was thought about and was considered worthy to receive something special. You are that special something or someone. We serve receivers by reminding them they are worthy. This is pleasing to the giver.

THE CRINGE

Have you ever heard it said, "I am unworthy, Lord," or " I am just a sinner saved by grace?" How preposterous! Nothing could be further from the truth. Scripture tell us that we are the apex of God's creation and were given delegated authority to be fruitful, multiply, replenish, subdue and have dominion over the works of his hand. I do not know of anyone who would spend time and energy creating something as majestic, magnificent and beautiful as the universe, and then hand it over to someone unworthy and incapable to manage.

I cringe when I hear such fallacy. Even in man's fallen state, he is worthy. The gifts of God are without repentance. When my children act out of character, I do not think of them as unworthy. I have a solution for that: mercy and truth. Why? My intent is not to focus on what they did wrong, but rather on them getting it right. For example, when one of my children mistreats the other, I do not think of that child as bad. I remind that child that he or she is family, and family love and look out for each other.

DISMISSING THE FALLACY OF UNWORTHY

Jesus is a master story teller. He is well known for telling parables. It's his way of conveying simple truth in a loving and non-threatening way. He knows that facts tell, but stories sell. He uses stories such as the lost sheep and the lost coin to express how precious we are to our Heavenly Father. He uses the word "until" in these stories to illustrate the Father's relentless love toward us. The "until" factor is not for the unworthy, but for worthy people and worthy ideals.

LOVE VERSES

Here are some love verses to settle the unworthy fallacy once and for all. You be the judge.

> *For God so loved the world, that he gave his only begotten Son, that whosoever believeth in him should not perish, but have everlasting life.*

For God sent not his Son into the world to condemn the world; but that the world through him might be saved. —**Apostle John**

In my Father's house are many mansions: if it were not so, I would have told you. I go to prepare a place for you. And if I go and prepare a place for you, I will come again, and receive you unto myself; that where I am, there you may be also. —**Jesus**

Whatever you desire, when you pray(ask), believe you receive them, and you shall have them. —**Jesus**

I will praise thee; for I am fearfully and wonderfully made: marvellous are thy works; and that my soul knoweth right well. —**David**

And I saw a new heaven and a new earth: for the first heaven and the first earth were passed away; and there was no more sea. And I John saw the holy city, new Jerusalem, coming down from God out of heaven, prepared as a bride adorned for her husband. And I heard a great voice out of heaven saying, Behold, the tabernacle of God is with men, and he will dwell with them, and they shall be his people, and God himself shall be with them, and be their God.

And God shall wipe away all tears from their eyes; and there shall be no more death, neither sorrow, nor crying, neither shall there be any more pain: for the former things are passed away. And he that sat upon the throne said, Behold, I make all things new. And he said unto me, Write: for these words are true and faithful. —**John, the Revelator**

THE PSYCHOLOGY OF WORTHY

Being worthy is not a mental ascent, an affirmation or a mantra one chants, but a characteristic of the divine nature in all of us. When

I think about God, I imagine all things good in infinite abundance, all things beautiful in infinite abundance, all things lovely in infinite abundance. Truly, the end of any phrase associated with God will most likely end with "...in infinite abundance."

Growing up and not being privilege to the lifestyle of the rich and famous had a temporary impact on my belief system concerning my worthiness. There were plenty of false evidences to convince me I was not worthy, such as not having enough food, clothing, or education. However, looking at the night sky with what seemed to be millions of stars was enough to remind me of how worthy I am. My belief as a child was that each star in the heavens was a representation of all the people on Earth. I would look for the brightest one and say, "That's me; that's my star."

I always knew I was a star — always. I believed it so much that I would push myself to be the brightest in the classroom, the fastest on the track, the best on the soccer field. That star fell mightily when my high school classmate, Gina, scored a goal in world class fashion by striking the ball through my legs. I was the laughing stock of the class for days. "How could you allow a girl to score on you like that?" my classmates would tease.

It's funny what we remember from our childhood. What can I say? It was an embarrassing moment for me. But little did I know that you do not have to try to become a star...you just have to be. You see, a star gets its illumination from the sun. If you and I are to be the stars that we are, then all we need is a relationship with the Son.

Chapter Six
THE CONDEMNATION SCRIPT

Prayer

Lord, we thank you that there is no condemnation to those who are in Christ Jesus, who walk not according to their senses but according to the Spirit. Amen

I grew up in rural Jamaica in the sleepy town of Castle Kelly St. Ann. It was the kind of town where everyone knew your name, and your business. I recall the local church being the only regular place of entertainment, except for the occasional movie night at a local grocery that used one of its rooms for community events. Castle Kelly was a bustling slave trade town in its heyday when Jamaica was under British rule. Remnants of plantation houses are still there today.

In our town, the local jailbird was Quintana. He was a tall, stout, muscular man. He seemed to be in and out of prison every few months. I remember him saying he felt better being in jail because that was where his friends where. He seemed happy when he was out, but a part of him had a longing to go back. Quintana's behavior, in clinical terms, is described as the Persister.

Shaad Maruna, In his book "Making Good: How ex-convicts reform their lives," says Persisters are the kind of people who will tell you they are sick and tired of doing crime, sick and tired of their life situation, but are also quick to attribute their situation to adverse circumstances which they believe to be out of their control. As such, they will continue their deviant behaviors, blaming their situation on poverty, drugs and a lack of education and job opportunities. Maruna states that these persistent offenders express themselves through what he calls a Condemnation Script. They make sense of their lives in terms of blocked opportunities and insurmountable obstacles, consistently communicating a sense of doom and hopelessness.

> ### Food for Thought
>
> *You are worthy to live a life free from condemnation. Don't allow your condemning thoughts to sabotage your dreams, visions and goals.*

SELF-IMPOSED PRISON

You may not be in and out of a physical prison, but I am sure we all have been there mentally and psychologically. It is the place where we settle. We call it the comfort zone. We don't see the need or benefit of making a change even though we know our lives stink living that way.

For example, you know it is time to quit smoking and you have tried many times to quit, but to no avail, so you conclude that it is your lot in life. You say, "I am a smoker and I will be that way until I die." That is bull secretion! You are worthy of a fresh breath, fresh smelling clothes, a healthy heart, lungs, liver, bladder, larynx...you name it. You are worthy of giving your significant other the most passionate kiss without him or her tasting nicotine or ashes. You are worthy of better use of the money you spend on smoke.

TOXIC RELATIONSHIPS CONDEMNATION SCRIPT

I am writing and reading my own mail, so I might as well send you a copy. Toxic relationships to me are the ones that slowly take your energy, your dreams, your goals, the vision you have for your life. They start out fantastic, but over time develop into agents of death.

Tamara Star wrote an article in the Huffington Post entitled "Seven Habits of Chronically Unhappy People." She prefaced the article by stating that we all have bad days. However, the difference between a happy and an unhappy life is how often and how long we stay there. This struck a nerve with me because these people are not bad or mean. In fact, oftentimes they are caring and sweet. However, they are people who tend to define their lives by the negatives. This in and of itself makes them candidates for toxic relationships.

Unhappy people's default belief is that life is hard and, as such, they see themselves as victims of life and stay stuck in the "look what happen to me " attitude instead of finding a way through and out of their situation.

Unhappy people believe most people can't be trusted. They have the stranger danger syndrome. This behavior closes doors on connections outside of their inner circle and drastically reduces the chance of meeting new friends. If you are with someone who is (or if you are) distrusting of others, you will find your sphere of influence increasingly shrinking. You can't be a world changer with that attitude. World changers need people to help them accomplish their vision.

Unhappy people focus on what is wrong with the world. They are afraid of accommodating anything good; this to them is nothing but a distraction. Happy people keep it in perspective and know the rule: be not overcome with evil, but overcome evil with good.

Unhappy people are jealous. They believe someone's good fortune steals from their own. They have what Solomon called a bad eye. They believe there is not enough goodness for everyone. Happy people have a good eye and believe in abundance, more than enough for everyone.

Unhappy people are worrisome and fearful. They are preoccupied with what could go wrong versus what might go right. They don't know happy people look at the same situation and feel it, but make the decision not to live it. That's what Jesus did: **"for the joy set before him he endured the cross."** If worry and fear affect you, start by confessing **"God did not give me a spirit of fear but of love power and a sound mind."**

Unhappy people gossip and complain constantly. They are what I call "past tense," always uptight about the past. The hardships of their lives are the conversation of choice. When they run out of things to say about themselves, they turn to other people's lives and gossip.

IDENTIFYING YOUR CONDEMNATION SCRIPT

What does your condemnation script sound like? Here is how to find out. Take a blank piece of paper and write everything that comes to your mind. Write everything you have been saying to yourself about why you cannot live your dream. Let it flow. Don't stop and don't question it. Just write to your heart's content. You deserve to know what that script is. When finished, take a few minutes to read it aloud. Now you know what your script is.

Now listen to me carefully.

Take your script and burn it. You are worthy to live a life free from condemnation.

WISDOM FROM THE KUNG FU MASTER

I like watching karate movies, especially the old ones. You know the kind – where you could see lips moving followed by sound a year later. The great Bruce Lee is my favorite karate movie actor. His swagger serves to remind us that one does not have to be huge to pack a big punch.

In the movie "Enter the Dragon," Bruce Lee fights the enemy in a mirrored room; the irony is he could only see his reflection. Needless to say, he was getting his butt kicked until he remembered these words from his karate master: "The enemy hides behind images and illusions. Destroy the image and you will break the enemy." WOW!

Similarly, in 2 Corinthians 10:3-6, it states:

For though we walk in the flesh we do not war after the flesh: For the weapons of our warfare are not carnal but mighty through God for the pulling down of strongholds; casting down imaginations and every high thing that exalt itself against the knowledge of God and bringing into captivity every thought to the obedience of Christ; and having all readiness to revenge all disobedience, when your obedience is fulfilled.

Simply put, fighting and winning the battle over our condemning thoughts is not physical, but spiritual.

Chapter Seven
BE DESERVING

Prayer

Lord, I thank you for teaching me that I am deserving of all the promises in your word; otherwise you would not have made them. I set myself in agreement with you and your word and with humility partake of your Divine nature. Amen.

In scripture, we are told that we have what we say and do. This statement implies that we are to be a people of vision rather than sight. Sight looks at the way things are while vision looks at things the way they should or could be. How do we know what we deserve? The Bible is clear when it tells us that the gifts of God are without repentance, and that every good gift is from above and comes from the Father above in whom there is no shadow of turning. You and I are deserving of everything our Heavenly Father gives.

Food for Thought

Deserving people take initiative.

WHAT ARE THESE PROMISES? CAN WE HAVE THEM ALL?

The promises of God are yes, yes and amen. You and I are deserving of every promise the Father makes to us. Jesus says, **"All that belongs to the Father is mine. That is why I said the Spirit will receive from me what he will make known to you. My Father will give you whatever you ask in my name. Until now you have not asked for anything in my name. Ask and you will receive, and your joy will be complete."**

King David gives us an insight of what some of these daily promises are in Psalm 103. For instance, there's a promise of forgiveness of all your sins and healing for all of your diseases. There's a promise of divine protection, and the promise of love and mercy. There's a promise of provision of good things that leads to the renewal of our bodies, and there is a promise of a legacy of love for those who fear him. There is a promise of being crowned with love and compassion, and there is a promise of our deepest desires being satisfied with good things. There is even a promise of God's righteousness to your children and grandchildren.

HOW DO WE ACTIVATE THESE PROMISES?

The word of God is like a mirror. We look into it to see who we are and what we are deserving of, and then we do it. As James 1: 22-24 clearly states: "Do not merely listen to the word, and so deceive yourselves. Do what it says. Anyone who listens to the word but does not do what it says is like someone who looks at his face in a mirror and, after looking at himself, goes away and immediately forgets what he looks like."

Jesus demonstrates how to be deserving

[14]Jesus returned to Galilee in the power of the Spirit, and news about him spread through the whole countryside. He was teaching in their synagogues, and everyone praised him. He went to Nazareth, where he had been brought up, and on the Sabbath day he went into the

synagogue, as was his custom. He stood up to read, [17] and the scroll of the prophet Isaiah was handed to him. Unrolling it, he found the place where it is written:

[18] "The Spirit of the Lord is on me, because he has anointed me to proclaim good news to the poor. He has sent me to proclaim freedom for the prisoners and recovery of sight for the blind, to set the oppressed free, to proclaim the year of the Lord's favor."[f]

[20] Then he rolled up the scroll, gave it back to the attendant and sat down. The eyes of everyone in the synagogue were fastened on him. [21] He began by saying to them, "Today this scripture is fulfilled in your hearing." [22] All spoke well of him and were amazed at the gracious words that came from his lips. "Isn't this Joseph's son?" they asked. [23] Jesus said to them, "Surely you will quote this proverb to me: 'Physician, heal yourself!' And you will tell me, 'Do here in your hometown what we have heard that you did in Capernaum.'" [24] "Truly I tell you," he continued, "no prophet is accepted in his hometown. [25] I assure you that there were many widows in Israel in Elijah's time, when the sky was shut for three and a half years and there was a severe famine throughout the land. [26] Yet Elijah was not sent to any of them, but to a widow in Zarephath in the region of Sidon. [27] And there were many in Israel with leprosy[g] in the time of Elisha the prophet, yet not one of them was cleansed—only Naaman the Syrian."

[28] All the people in the synagogue were furious when they heard this. [29] They got up, drove him out of the town, and took him to the brow of the hill on which the town was built, in order to throw him off the cliff. [30] But he walked right through the crowd and went on his way.
Luke 4:14-28

Now, let's break this down.

Jesus went into the temple, found the scripture that described him and read it. Jesus said, "I am the one this scripture is talking about," and sat down. This was very important because a prophet is without honor in his own country. The people who knew you back then would take a longer time to accept the changes in your life. I call this familiar spirits. These types of spirits are trapped in your past and cannot recognize the work that God has completed in you. Now, can you imagine what people who knew Jesus back then were saying? Here's how it probably went:

You mean Joseph the carpenter's son? Yes, sir.

You mean Mary's baby boy? Yes, madam.

You, the messiah? Yes.

Get out of here! I think I will.

Jesus left them knowing and declaring who he was. It made some glad and it made some mad, but there was no recanting on His part. You and I will have to do the same if we are to walk out and live in the promises of our Heavenly Father. Those experiences are normal to deserving people. You will have to get used to it. So, here's my formula for activating God's promise:

Formula for Activating God's Promise

1. Find the promise.
2. Read the promise aloud.
3. Declare the promise.
4. Believe that you receive the promise.

Let me demonstrate how this formula can be used to activate the promise for healing and provision.

Activating Healing

The promises of God are more than treasure to me. They are delegated authority I can activate at a moment's notice. If there are symptoms of sickness in our bodies we can do what Jesus did.

So, let's use the formula to activate healing.

> **Using formula to Activate Healing**
>
> 1. Open the scriptures and find where it is written about healing: By His stripes I am healed.
> 2. Read it aloud: by His stripes I am healed.
> 3. Declare: I am healed by His stripe.
> 4. Sit down: That settles it.

Now imagine having this conversation with either yourself or loved ones after your declaration:

How do you feel? Terrible, but I am healed.

You can barely move. Yes, but I am healed.

You can hardly breathe. Yes, but I am healed.

That's religious hogwash. Whatever, I am healed.

Notice that we are using the past tense. This is what our Heavenly Father planned for us before the foundation of the world. It is common knowledge that every company that produces a product has a service department. They are there in case something goes wrong with the product. There were people getting healed before Jesus was born. That showed it was always available. His death, burial and resurrection are tangible evidence given so that we might believe.

Activating Provision

Let's change gears and focus on how to activate provision. If I sense a lack of provision coming on, I go to the mirror of the word and use the above formula to activate provision.

> **EXAMPLE:**
>
> *I see in the word:* My God shall supply all your needs according to His riches in glory by Christ Jesus.
>
> *I see in the word:* Give and it shall be given to you good measure press down shaken together and running over shall men give into your bosom.
>
> *I read them aloud:* My God shall supply all your needs according to His riches in glory by Chris Jesus, give and it shall be given to you good measure press down shaken together and running over shall men give into your bosom.
>
> *I declare:* Father, I believe you are my source; I sew a financial seed in accordance with your word. I believe all my needs are met, I believe I receive my provision. In Jesus' name.
>
> *Sit down:* Then I rest in faith believing I receive what I ask.

Believing and deservedness are a must when using this formula. Most people believe the promises of God but do not see themselves as deserving. Let's here from the Apostle John on how to deal with this issue:

> [19]And hereby we know that we are**(deserving)** of the truth, and shall assure our hearts before him. [20]For if our heart condemn us, God is greater than our heart, and knoweth all things. [21]Beloved, if our heart condemn us not, then have we confidence toward God. 22And whatsoever we ask, we receive of him, because we keep his commandments, and do those things that are pleasing in his sight.[23]And this is his commandment, That we should believe on the name of his Son Jesus Christ, and love one another, as he gave us commandment. 1 John 3:19-23

First, John tells us that we are to know and agree with the truth. Truth means our eternal spiritual reality. This realty comes from our connectivity to God. That is why Jesus said "I am truth." He was always conscious of his connection with the father (source). Is God healthy and wealthy? Yes! Then so are we. Our dreams of health and abundance are clues that this reality exist for us.

Second, He told us that if our heart does not condemn us then we have confidence toward God and whatever we ask we receive of Him. Asking, then, is not hoping, but knowing that our requests and answers are preprogrammed in God. For example, our cell phones are preprogrammed to make and receive calls. As such, we know what to do to make and receive a phone call. This is because these features are of the cell phone.

Third, John told us that if our heart condemn us then we must take it to God, the source who is greater than our hearts and know all things at all times. He will give us the assurance that we are deserving of Him. This means fixing our malfunction, which is a condemning heart. In the field of electrical engineering, this is called a BIST (Built-In-Self-Test). This mechanism allows a machine to test itself. The benefits are high reliability and low repair cycle time. You can spear yourself a trip and expenses seeking human intervention by submitting yourself to the Father for diagnosis and repair. Do you remember Jesus saying that it's the Father (source) who does the work? That is what he meant.

Lastly, John told us we please the father by giving him exactly what he commanded, and this is his commandment: that we should believe on the name of his Son Jesus Christ, and love one another. When you and I don't feel deserving, we are commanded to believe that Jesus, the Messiah, our savior, is deserving. Therefore, we must activate all requests through him.

FRUSTRATING THE GRACE OF GOD

To deny the word of God the opportunity to work in our lives is what the Apostle Paul called "frustrating the Grace." He said, "I do not frustrate the grace of God: For if righteousness comes by the law, then Christ is dead in vain." The work is already done, for it is the Father who does the work. God's grace is available to us for all of life's circumstances. The Grace that saves is the grace that forgives. The grace that forgives is the grace that heals. The grace that heals is the grace that provides. The grace that provides is the grace that delivers. The grace that delivers is the grace that comforts.

BE FEARLESS

When I say be fearless, I am not implying that you need to get to a place where there is no fear whatsoever. What I say is what I mean: Fear less. Get in the habit of minimizing the crippling effects of fear in your life. We know and we understand that fear is the enemy of progress. Scripture teaches us that ignorance is one of the main forces behind it. Specifically, in Isaiah 41:10, it clearly states:

> **"So do not fear, for I am with you; do not be dismayed, for I am your God. I will strengthen you and help you; I will uphold you with my righteous right hand."**

God said through his prophet that there is no need to fear because he is with us. What that means to me is that I have an all-powerful, all knowing and present-everywhere force at my disposal. What I don't know, He knows, what I can't see, He sees. What I can't do, he does.

I remember a time in our home when the older children would chase the younger ones around the house with what they termed "monster faces." The younger children would run and scream, sometimes even cry. One day my daughter came running, crying and screaming towards me with a look of terror in her eyes. She said, "Daddy, hide me, they are making mean faces at me." Soon after, her brothers came running toward us with mean and ugly monster faces. However, this time I was with her, her tears had dried; the look of terror was gone. As we move toward her brothers,

I could see them backing up. I looked down at my daughter and there she was making mean and ugly monster faces at them with a sheepish grin. That is what recognition of the presence of almighty God will do for you. It will embolden you. It will put the fear in that which you fear. Don't let fear stop you from living your dreams. Successful people create opportunities. They move in spite of fear, while failures wait for opportunities. Be fearless; you are deserving.

Chapter Eight
BE GREAT

Prayer
I thank you, Father for the reminder that anyone who aspires to be great must seek to serve as many of his fellow man as he possibly can. I submit to that word through obedient action and gladly proclaim that I am great. Amen.

THE GREATEST IS THE SERVANT OF ALL

For the Son of man did not come to be served, but to serve and to give his life a ransom for many. In the church world, the concept of serving is highly encouraged; members are constantly called upon to lend a helping hand in the daily operation of their local church, especially on the weekend when their local congregations meet. Church members are asked to serve as greeters, ushers, choir members, child care givers and Sunday school teachers. Based on my experience, there seems to be a faithful few who volunteer week in and week out, some do it joyfully while others are flat burnt out. What would cause some to feel burnout doing God's work?

Here is my theory: most people do not serve from the overflow of their lives, they serve from the almost empty reservoir of their lives. They operate from the 'have to' instead of the 'want to' mentality. How many times do you hear someone say, "I have to go to church," "I have to go to that meeting," "I have to preach?" These are all slavery expressions. God's word tells us that he loves a cheerful giver, but why would people give cheerfully? The obvious answer is because they want to or, better yet, they know that giving activates the law of receiving. It is in giving that we receive. Serving is a type of giving, but nowhere in scripture are we commanded to do it for free. That type of serving is referred to as volunteering and comes from the "want to" or "get to" mentality. I say this because it is my suspicion why so little of us serve. Even on the job, people do not serve well. There are excuses of not being paid enough, not recognized enough or the task is not a part of their job description. The list goes on and on.

Serving is more than just showing up for an assignment. It entails careful consideration and preparation for the client. I believe God is served best when we serve each other. After all, we are his children, and there is no greater joy than seeing sibling loving and caring for each other. I am a living witness to that truth.

THE STORY OF THE STOLEN CAR

When our daughter was born, I wanted to name her Tatiana. Her mother was in such opposition that she cried and threatened me about using that name. I thought it was a fitting name for a girl, but she thought it was just, well…in her own words…ugly. My apology to all the Tatiana's out there. After much deliberation, we named her Gabreial Alexis Grant.

I thought the name Tatiana belonged in the family, so I decided to give that name to our 1995 Toyota Camry. Tatiana served us well for many years. However, in 2012, she was stolen. I filed a police report. A year later the local police called to give us the news that Tatiana was found behind a local hotel, and they told us where we may retrieve her. Needless to say, I was a happy man. I called the local salvage yard and inquired about what they needed me to bring as proof that she was mine. They gave me a list of things, one of them being money for storage. I gathered the documents as fast as I could and brought it to them. I was then able to drive her home...reunited, and it felt so good.

I told the story for in it lies the three keys to serving well. These keys are:

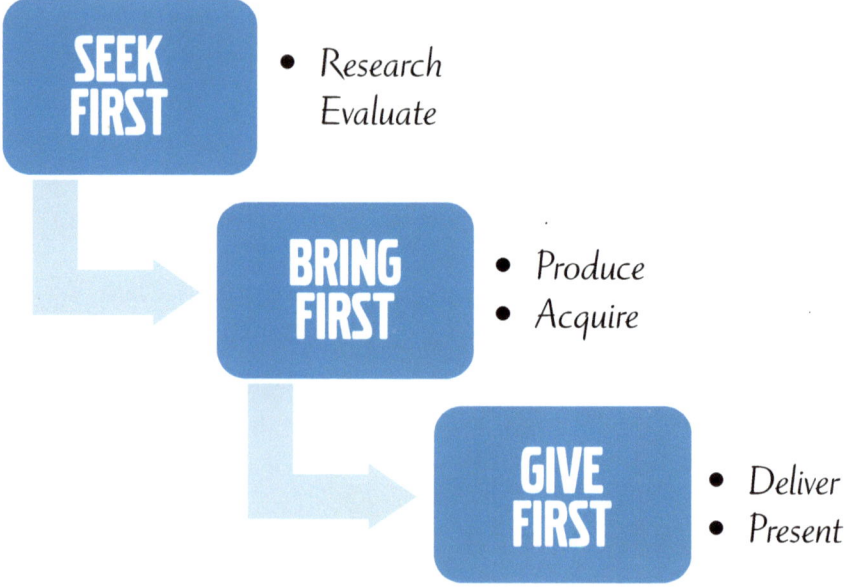

Seek First

In order to reunite with Tatiana, I needed to know what was required by the salvage yard. In a similar way, to have the best shot at attracting and retaining clients – or dare I say, unite with them – one needs to know what their needs are. It can be as basic as asking a few questions to as complex as a full-blown market research. The Seek First principle is effective and transferable to all endeavors of human interaction. You see, a life of service is pursued by those who believe they are worthy. The doctor has to thoroughly examine the patient before he prescribes the right medicine. A business person will have to do his or her due diligence before buying a business. And a family will ensure a house meets their needs before purchasing it. Worthy people are in the habit of seeking first.

Millions of people enroll in universities and other educational institutions each year. For many, it was what they were told to do. However, for the worthy it is what they must do. While others seek an education, the deserving seek an opportunity for which they must be educated. History has taught us that some of the most influential people of our day were college dropouts. In their own words, they did so because the pace of the formal, organized education lagged the opportunity. People like the late Steve Jobs, Michael Dell, Bill Gates and Oprah Winfrey, just to name a few.

Not all opportunities require a formal education, so the deserving must be discerning. The field of sports and entertainment are the ones that immediately come to mind. What are the opportunities you wish to pursue? Do they require a formal or non-formal education? Why or why not? Remember the rule: Seek first and educate for the opportunity; that's what deserving people do.

Bring First

Every year millions of new products are introduced to the market place. Most, if not all of them, were developed from some sort of market research data. These companies are so focused on the opportunity that they are willing to spend thousands of man hours and millions of dollars in product development. All of this effort and resource is behind one belief: If they do not bring it, we the consumer will not see it to buy it. If I ever wanted to reunite with Tatiana, I had to bring all the required documents, including cash. What do the opportunities you seek require of you? Do you have them ready to deliver if called upon? Why or why not? If you do not know, then it is time to find out and bring it. That's what worthy people do.

Give First

It is said that most products we see in stores are not paid for until we, the consumers, purchase them. This means that the whole supply chain is at a deficit until that product is sold. That is the kind of risk that worthy people take every day. They know if they are to be great then they must give first.

The farmer knows this reality too well. If he needs a harvest, he must plant a seed. The athlete, entertainer, business man, student or whomever it may be must give time, energy, blood, sweat and tears before they can call themselves qualified and worthy of the opportunity. That is what risk taking is all about. The upside must drastically outweigh the downside, otherwise it is called foolishness. Remember the rule: Give First. That is one of the traits of the greats. Deserving people have no problem giving first.

EXTRAPOLATE

Now, let's apply this principle to some key areas of your life.

Do you want a great relationship with your spouse, children or loved ones? Then seek first, bring first, give first.

Do you want a great body mind relationship with yourself? Then seek first, bring first, give first.

Do you want a healthy relationship with your finances? Then seek first, bring first, give first.

Do you wish to start a great relationship with your creator? Then seek first, bring first, give first.

I recall giving all the required documents, including cash, to the person at the service window at that salvage yard. I remember being escorted to the back of the building where the vehicle was parked. I recall the joy I felt reuniting with Tatiana. That is what the greats do. They know there are opportunities to be reunited, and they don't mind serving their way into them. They know they must seek first, bring first and give first.

Chapter Nine
SUCCESS HABITS OF THE WORTHY

Prayer

Father, I thank you that I am not without hope because you have shown through our ancestors that you're a good God and that if you came through for them you will come through for me because you are the same yesterday, today and forever. Amen

SUCCESS IS FIRST SPIRITUAL

By faith, we understand that the universe was formed at God's command – so what is seen was not made out of what was visible. Then God said, "Let the land produce vegetation: Seedbearing plants and trees on the land that bear fruit with seed in it, according to their various kinds. And it was so. The land produced vegetation: plants bearing seed according to their kinds and trees bearing fruit with seed in it according to their kinds. And God saw that it was good. And there was evening, and there was morning—the third day."

Intrinsically, every seed is designed to produce a specific fruit, and every fruit is designed to produce a specific seed. The seed contains the genetic makeup to produce that specific fruit every single time. We could then say that it's the habit of a specific seed to produce a specific fruit. For example, it is the habit of an apple seed to produce apples, and the habit of a mango seed to produce mangoes. Their actions are repeatable and, therefore, predictable. For by their fruit you shall know them.

We behave the way we do because of our habitual thoughts and actions, with our thoughts being the catalyst behind our actions... for as a man thinks and continues to think, in his heart, so is he. This is genius to me. I know what to do if I want to change any habit. The Creator has given us this working model from the beginning and has equipped us with the capacity to develop habits using thoughts and actions. Below is the working model:

$$Habit = \frac{(Thoughts + Corresponding\ Actions)}{Time}$$

Some people say we can develop a new habit in 21 continuous days. Some say 30 days. As for me, I don't care. I like to keep it simple and focus on the main thing which is developing new habits that serves my vision, dreams and goals. So if 21 days or 30 days should pass and the new habit is not formed, I don't quit. I don't say it does not work. I continue because I know I am one day closer. You are invited to do the same. The results are predictable, but the benefits are life changing.

> ### The Principle of Habit Force
> *Successful people are in the habit of developing habits that support their visions, dreams and goals.*

The habit of habits is the foundation behind every success and failure. It is said that the difference between successful people and those who fail is that successful people are in the habit of doing what failures don't like to do. It is also found that successful people are similar to those who fail in that they don't like doing the things they do either. However, they are in the habit of focusing on pleasing results, while failures are in the habit of focusing on pleasing methods. If the habits you currently have do not give you the results you desire, then a change in habit that supports your desire is required. You are worthy, and your desires are worthy of you. Program yourself to attract those desires.

DEFINITE AIM

Worthy people are in the habit of being clear about what they want. They understand that we think in pictures. The clearer the picture, the easier it is to attain your goals. Clarity attracts others to help you fulfill your goals. The Bible says it best: "…write the vision and engrave it so plainly upon tablets that everyone who passes may be able to read it easily and quickly as he hastens by." (Habakkuk 2:2) The bottom line is that desire always has a picture in mind. Be clear.

THE MASTER MIND

Worthy people are in the habit of forming master minds. The master mind is defined as two or more people harmoniously coming together and working toward a definite purpose. The master mind, then, is separate, different and more powerful than the individual minds.

The original master mind is that of the God head (Father, Son, and Spirit) harmoniously coming together to create the world: And God said let us make man in our image and in our likeness and let them have dominion over the universe. Adam and Eve (the first husband and wife relationship) being in the image and likeness of God were designed to form a master mind with the definite purpose of managing God's creation. Forming master minds automatically attracts the Creator: For wherever two or three are gathered touching anything concerning me there I am in the midst. We were not designed to create alone, but to be co-creator with God.

Here is a word of caution to spouses or significant others: if you sense or know that your minds are antagonistic toward each other and the vibration is off, make it your duty to align yourselves before forming a master mind around any definite aim you may have. If this is not possible at the time, then find people you can agree and work with. Don't allow one person to sabotage your goals and dreams.

SELF-CONFIDENCE

Marcus Garvey claims: "If you have no confidence in self you are twice defeated in the race of life but with confidence you have won even before you have started." It is said that one of the biggest enemies to defeat is fear. Men and women of great intellect have succumbed to this crippling force. In the book, *Think and Grow Rich*, authored by Napoléon Hill, there are six basic fears:

1. A fear of poverty
2. A fear of old age
3. A fear of criticism
4. A fear of the loss of love
5. A fear of sickness
6. A fear of death

At some point in time, anyone who aspires to be great or to pursue a worthy ideal will have to face at least one of these fears. As a result of this, worthy people are always in the habit of overcoming fear and, in the process, develop and build their self-confidence. Self-confidence is simply believing you can. It is the ability to see oneself as the image of the creator. The Bible teaches "That God did not give us a spirit of fear but of love of power and of a sound mind."

You are worthy; develop the habit of being self-confident.

SAVINGS

To save, one must first earn. Therefore, the first thing worthy people do is decide how much money they would like to earn. Next, they develop an action plan by which they may attain that objective. Finally, they work that plan. For example, if I want to earn $40,000 a month, I need a plan for $10,000 a week, $2,000 a day assuming a five-day work week. This process may involve changing habits, developing new ones or overcoming certain fears. If criticism is one of your fears, then you will have to develop a new self-image and mindset that affirms you are worthy of the money because you serve others. If you have a fear of poverty, then you will have to start thinking of abundance and prosperity as being your birth right. Now that you are earning, you can form the habit of putting aside a portion; this may be a fixed amount or a percentage. As your earnings increase, so will your savings. If you are in debt, then an exit strategy must be included in your earning plan. No one should be a slave to such tyranny. I have been there and, to a lesser extent, still am. Debt robs you of joy, but most importantly, it robs your creativity because most of your time is spent thinking about it. No wonder Jesus told us we cannot serve God and money. To serve God, one must be in the habit of creating. You are worthy of a lifestyle of abundance, so develop a habit of saving.

INITIATIVE AND LEADERSHIP

In the book *Think and Grow Rich*, Napoleon Hill states that self-confidence is a prerequisite to initiative and leadership because no one could become an efficient leader or take the initiative in any great undertaking without belief in himself or herself. He went on to say that leadership is essential for success and initiative, and is the very foundation upon which leadership is built. Therefore, initiative is as essential to success.

Initiative is the ability to do what needs to be done without being told. As such, you can never find a leader who has not acquired the habit of initiative because leadership is something you must invite yourself into. Initiative and leadership, then, is most vital to your chief aim. Otherwise, your chief aim is just a wish.

ENTHUSIASM (THE GOD WITHIN)

This is the state of mind that inspires and causes a person and those around him or her to take action. It is the single most important factor in the transference of a vision or a definite aim. Enthusiasm energizes you and the people around you, and will keep you pushing for your dreams when things around you are falling apart. If you keep being enthusiastic, it won't be long before the obstacles in your path give way. It has a way of changing the atmosphere around you. Have you ever gone to a church service all tired, beat up and dejected? Did you notice that it took only a few lively songs and a spirited sermon to get you rejuvenated? That's what enthusiasm can do for you.

The famous televangelist and pastor of Lakewood Church in Houston, Texas, Joel Osteen, said: "One of the main reasons that we lose our enthusiasm in life is because we become ungrateful… we let what was once a miracle become common to us. We get so accustomed to his (God) goodness it becomes a routine…" Get in the habit of being enthusiastic; it will keep you going long after your enemies are gone.

GOING THE EXTRA MILE

Doing more than you have to or doing something you did not have to do, and with an attitude of generosity, is the definition of going the extra mile. Giving of oneself in this way lifts the human spirit. All of humanity stands and applauds such gestures because it is an act that celebrates all of us. The heart grows tender when we extend ourselves beyond what's expected. Jesus told a story in Luke, Chapter 10, that illustrates this attitude:

The Parable of the Good Samaritan

[25]And behold, a lawyer stood up to put him to the test, saying, "Teacher, what shall I do to inherit eternal life?" [26]He said to him, "What is written in the Law? How do you read it?" [27]And he answered, "You shall love the Lord your God with all your heart and with all your soul and with all your strength and with all your mind, and your neighbor as yourself." [28]And he said to him, "You have answered correctly; do this, and you will live."

²⁹*But he, desiring to justify himself, said to Jesus, "And who is my neighbor?"* ³⁰ *Jesus replied, "A man was going down from Jerusalem to Jericho, and he fell among robbers, who stripped him and beat him and departed, leaving him half dead.* ³¹ *Now by chance a priest was going down that road, and when he saw him he passed by on the other side.* ³² *So likewise a Levite, when he came to the place and saw him, passed by on the other side.* ³³ *But a Samaritan, as he journeyed, came to where he was, and when he saw him, he had compassion.* ³⁴ *He went to him and bound up his wounds, pouring on oil and wine. Then he set him on his own animal and brought him to an inn and took care of him.* ³⁵ *And the next day he took out two denarii[a] and gave them to the innkeeper, saying, 'Take care of him, and whatever more you spend, I will repay you when I come back.'* ³⁶ *Which of these three, do you think, proved to be a neighbor to the man who fell among the robbers?"* ³⁷ *He said, "The one who showed him mercy." And Jesus said to him, "You go, and do likewise."*

Success and going the extra mile go hand in hand. With them, businesses and customers are lost or won. For most organizations, it is what distinguishes them from their competition. Do you go the extra mile? How does this serve you?

Chapter Ten
LEAD YOUR LIFE

> ### Prayer
> Lord, thank you for giving us free will to lead our lives successfully into whatever endeavors we so choose. We thank you for the wisdom, knowledge and understanding that you so graciously provide to help along the way. Heavenly Father, I ask you to give me and each person I have prayed for today Clarity of vision, Clarity of sight, Clarity of thought, Clarity of mind, Clarity of knowing and hearing your voice, so that we may lead the abundant life you so graciously provide. In Jesus' name. Amen.

MANDATES OF LEADERSHIP

Food for Thought
Character before compliment.

In order to lead an effective life, one must have a vision for his or her life. This constitutes a good self-image. How do you see yourself? How do you want others to see you?

The priority of self-image is character. A character is that which maintains its meaning and never changes. It has distinctive qualities that make it recognizable and differentiated. An excellent example of this is the letters and numbers that make up the English language: "A to Z" and "0 to 9." These alpha-numeric characters have been the same since their inception, and will continue to be that way. The obvious benefit of these characters is that we use them to communicate daily with no regard to them ever-changing. They have stood the test of time; reliable and trustworthy.

In a similar way, you and I were created to be a people who are consistent in nature, distinctive and differentiated. Who we are, what we say and what we do are one and the same. Character, therefore, ensures security and reliability, which lead ultimately to pleasure. It guarantees a solid foundation to build life on, effective communication is assured, you know what to expect, and you know the end from the beginning.

Character is not something we try to attain; it is part and parcel of who we are. The benefits are infinite. Activate yours today by standing in your personal power, declaring and being a person of character.

LEAD WITH YOUR LIFE

Once character is activated, you are ready to lead with your life. You become that positive, consistent example others can follow. Simply put, you become very attractive, sexy and irresistible. A word of caution: a person of character knows that there is no such thing as a private life. The letters of the alphabet are distinct, be they upper or lower case. Personally, I prefer big and bold. Be like Jesus and live out loud!

MANDATES OF LEADERSHIP

The Transformer series of comic books, toys and movies gives a vivid depiction of the statement made by Apostle Paul. He states, "Do not conform to the pattern of this world, but be transformed

by the renewing of your mind. Then you will be able to test and approve what God's will is-Good, Perfect and Pleasing." These giant robots are able to change and adjust, depending on the threatening environment they are in.

If they could not go through their obstacles, then they would change into objects that could go under, over or around the situation. That is exactly how you and I are created to lead our lives. God designed us to win in life every single time. If we are aware and are willing to activate our transforming abilities, then we will be able to test and prove the way he created us to be.

Here are the three mandatory power steps to follow when leading the transforming life:

STEP 1	STEP 2	STEP 3
• See things as they are, not worse (do not exaggerate).	• See things better than they are (get a vision for your life).	• Make it the way you envisioned it (go to work on your vision).

Remember, we are predestined for a good, pleasing, perfect result in the midst of trouble. Believe it, receive it, embrace it and share it.

Chapter Eleven
A CLOUD OF WITNESS

Prayer

Father, I thank you that I am not without hope because you have shown through our ancestors that you're a good God and that if you came through for them you will come through for me because you are the same yesterday, today and forever. Amen

---

The Principle of Modeling

The fastest way to success is role-modeling.

If there is one quality that stands out for people who see themselves worthy is that they have unwavering faith. They use the 'until factor' to achieve their worthy ideals. In other words, the outcome or the result is all that they see. All obstacles must give way. Their accomplishments are positive examples for us to follow. Let's hear what the Creator has to say about faith and the many people who benefitted from using it in their lives.

In Hebrews 11-12, it states:

Now faith is the substance of things hoped for, the evidence of things not seen. For by it the elders obtained a good report. Through faith we understand that the worlds were framed by the word of God, so that things which are seen were not made of things which do appear.

> **NO EGO** [Worthy people use the word of God to reclaim, reframe and rename their world].

By faith Abel offered unto God a more excellent sacrifice than Cain, by which he obtained witness that he was righteous, God testifying of his gifts: and by it he being dead yet speaketh. By faith Enoch was translated that he should not see death; and was not found, because God had translated him: for before his translation he had this testimony, that he pleased God. But without faith it is impossible to please him: for he that cometh to God must believe that he is, and that he is a rewarder of them that diligently seek him.

> **NO EGO** [The Worthy are more concerned with pleasing God than people, they know there is a reward on the other side of their faith.]

By faith Noah, being warned of God of things not seen as yet, moved with fear, prepared an ark to the saving of his house; by which he condemned the world, and became heir of the righteousness which is by faith.

> **NO EGO** [Worthy people do not allow fear to hinder their faith, they act in spite of it.]

By faith Abraham, when he was called to go out into a place which he should after receive for an inheritance, obeyed; and he went out, not knowing whither he went. By faith he sojourned in the land of promise, as in a strange country, dwelling in tabernacles with Isaac and Jacob, the heirs with him of the same promise: For he looked for a city which hath foundations, whose builder and maker is God.

> [Worthy people know that a word from God is enough.]

Through faith also Sara herself received strength to conceive seed, and was delivered of a child when she was past age, because she judged him faithful who had promised. Therefore sprang there even of one, and him as good as dead, so many as the stars of the sky in multitude, and as the sand which is by the sea shore innumerable.

> [Worthy people know that God is trustworthy, they know it's the father within that does the work.]

These all died in faith, not having received the promises, but having seen them afar off, and were persuaded of them, and embraced them, and confessed that they were strangers and pilgrims on the earth. For they that say such things declare plainly that they seek a country.

And truly, if they had been mindful of that country from whence they came out, they might have had opportunity to have returned. But now they desire a better country, that is, a heavenly: wherefore God is not ashamed to be called their God: for He hath prepared for them a city.

> [The worthy are more vision conscious than sight conscious.]

By faith Abraham, when he was tried, offered up Isaac: and he that had received the promises offered up his only begotten son, Of whom it was said, That in Isaac shall thy seed be called:

Accounting that God was able to raise him up, even from the dead; from whence also he received him in a figure.

> *[The worthy trust even when they don't understand.]*

By faith Isaac blessed Jacob and Esau concerning things to come. By faith Jacob, when he was a dying, blessed both the sons of Joseph; and worshipped, leaning upon the top of his staff. By faith Joseph, when he died, made mention of the departing of the children of Israel; and gave commandment concerning his bones.

> *[Worthy people are legacy and inheritance conscious.]*

By faith Moses, when he was born, was hid three months of his parents, because they saw he was a proper child; and they were not afraid of the king's commandment.

By faith Moses, when he was come to years, refused to be called the son of Pharaoh's daughter; Choosing rather to suffer affliction with the people of God, than to enjoy the pleasures of sin for a season; Esteeming the reproach of Christ greater riches than the treasures in Egypt: for he had respect unto the recompense of the reward.

> *[Worthy people are purpose driven.]*

By faith he forsook Egypt, not fearing the wrath of the king: for he endured, as seeing him who is invisible. Through faith he kept the Passover, and the sprinkling of blood, lest he that destroyed the firstborn should touch them. By faith they passed through the Red sea as by dry land: which the Egyptians assaying to do were drowned.

> *[The worthy can succeed where others fail, because they hear the voice of God.]*

By faith the walls of Jericho fell down, after they were compassed about seven days.

By faith the harlot Rahab perished not with them that believed not, when she had received the spies with peace.

> **NO EGO** *[Are you surprised, prostitutes are worthy people too!]*

And what shall I more say? For the time would fail me to tell of Gideon, and of Barak, and of Samson, and of Jephthae; of David also, and Samuel, and of the prophets: Who through faith subdued kingdoms, wrought righteousness, obtained promises, stopped the mouths of lions?

Quenched the violence of fire, escaped the edge of the sword, out of weakness were made strong, waxed valiant in fight, turned to flight the armies of the aliens.

Women received their dead raised to life again: and others were tortured, not accepting deliverance; that they might obtain a better resurrection: And others had trial of cruel mockings and scourgings, yes, moreover of bonds and imprisonment: They were stoned, they were sawn asunder, were tempted, were slain with the sword: they wandered about in sheepskins and goatskins; being destitute, afflicted, tormented; (Of whom the world was not worthy.) They wandered in deserts, and in mountains, and in dens and caves of the earth.

And these all, having obtained a good report through faith, received not the promise:

God having provided some better thing for us, that they without us should not be made perfect.

> **NO EGO** *[There are too many examples of worthy people for you to punk out. Get a grip, "You are too legit to quit." — MC Hammer]*

Wherefore seeing we also are compassed about with so great a cloud of witnesses, let us lay aside every weight, and the sin which doth so easily beset us, and let us run with patience the race that is set before us, Looking unto Jesus the author and finisher of our faith; who for the joy that was set before him endured the cross, despising the shame, and is set down at the right hand of the throne of God.

> **NO EGO** *[Worthy people see the end from the beginning and therefore are not afraid of the process, they look for role models, do what they do in order that they may get the same results.]*

For consider him that endured such contradiction of sinners against himself, lest you be wearied and faint in your minds. You have not yet resisted unto blood, striving against sin.

And you have forgotten the exhortation which speaketh unto you as unto children, My son, despise not thou the chastening of the Lord, nor faint when thou art rebuked of him:

For whom the Lord loveth, he chasteneth, and scourgeth every son whom he receiveth. If you endure chastening, God dealeth with you as with sons; for what son is he whom the father chasteneth not? But if you be without chastisement, whereof all are partakers, then are you bastards, and not sons.

> **NO EGO** *[Worthy people seek out mentors, they do not have a 'Know-It All' attitude, they don't mind been corrected because they know it is to their benefit.]*

Furthermore we have had fathers of our flesh which corrected us, and we gave them reverence: shall we not much rather be in subjection unto the Father of spirits, and live? For they verily for a few days chastened us after their own pleasure; but he for our profit, that we might be partakers of his holiness.

Now, no chastening for the present seemeth to be joyous, but grievous: nevertheless afterward it yieldeth the peaceable fruit of righteousness unto them which are exercised thereby.

Wherefore lift up the hands which hang down, and the feeble knees; And make straight paths for your feet, lest that which is lame be turned out of the way; but let it rather be healed.

 [The worthy have no time to feel sorry for themselves.]

Follow peace with all men, and holiness without which no man shall see the Lord:

 [The worthy are people with integrity.]

Looking diligently lest any man fail of the grace of God; lest any root of bitterness springing up trouble you, and thereby many be defiled; Lest there be any fornicator, or profane person, as Esau, who for one morsel of meat sold his birthright.

[Worthy people are constantly checking their thought life, they can't afford to harbor any grudges. Anything that take them away from their focus is not welcome.]

For you know how that afterward, when he would have inherited the blessing, he was rejected: for he found no place of repentance, though he sought it carefully with tears.

For you are not come unto the mount that might be touched, and that burned with fire, nor unto blackness, and darkness, and tempest, And the sound of a trumpet, and the voice of words; which voice they that heard entreated that the word should not be spoken to them any more:(For they could not endure that which was commanded, And if so much as a beast touch the mountain, it shall be stoned, or thrust through with a dart: And so terrible was the sight, that Moses said, I exceedingly fear and quake:)

> **NO EGO** *[Fear of messing up is a thing of the past, You are welcome to talk to God when you like, he won't bite.]*

But you are come unto mount Zion and unto the city of the living God, the heavenly Jerusalem, and to an innumerable company of angels, To the general assembly and church of the firstborn, which are written in heaven, and to God the Judge of all, and to the spirits of just men made perfect, And to Jesus the mediator of the new covenant, and to the blood of sprinkling, that speaketh better things than that of Abel.

> **NO EGO** *[Worthy people know, it is all about Jesus, they know that they can ask for big things boldly because they are in covenant.]*

See that you refuse not him that speaketh. For if they escaped not who refused him that spake on earth, much more shall not we escape, if we turn away from him that speaketh from heaven: Whose voice then shook the earth: but now he hath promised, saying, Yet once more I shake not the earth only, but also heaven. And this word, yet once more, signifieth the removing of those things that are shaken, as of things that are made, that those things which cannot be shaken may remain. Wherefore we receiving a kingdom which cannot be moved, let us have grace, whereby we may serve God acceptably with reverence and godly fear: For our God is a consuming fire.

> **NO EGO** *[Worthy people like the real deal, they are not into fake or fluff. They are concerned and consumed with things that will last through eternity.]*

We have heard from several witnesses, and now there's overwhelming evidence to return a verdict...all rise. In the case of Satan vs. the People of the Kingdom of God, I, the Creator, find the defendants not guilty of being unworthy.

Chapter Twelve
THE X FACTOR

Prayer

Lord, my dreams are so big, you gave them to me. I know you are the God who knows the end from the beginning, so I thank you today that through the spirit, you will guide my every step and provide the resource necessary as I seek to honor you in the fulfillment of my dreams. Amen.

The Principle of Partnership

God invites us to invite him into our affairs through prayer.

God is present to help in times of trouble, and he invites us to invite him into our affairs through prayer. Prayer is the key to activating the resources of Heaven to work on our behalf. It's important to understand that with God, all things are possible. History has taught us that one person can make a difference in the world working in conjunction with their Creator:

- o With God, Noah built an ark and saved his family while a flood destroyed the entire world.

- With God, Abraham Lincoln designed, developed and deliver a document that would henceforth and forever free the American slaves.
- With God, Dr. Martin Luther King Jr. was able to influence the American congress to pass civil rights laws, giving blacks access to their rights as citizens.
- With God, Moses delivered the Israelites from slavery in Egypt, crossed the Red Sea and brought them to the edge of the promise land.
- With God, Joseph was able to withstand his brothers' hatred, survive prison, became the prime minister of Egypt and devised a strategy that saved the world from starvation.
- With God, Nelson Mandela fought apartheid, survived 27 years in prison and became the first black president of his beloved country, South Africa.
- With God, Jesus survived Herod's assassination, overcame temptation, turned water into wine, fed five thousand families with a 2-piece fish dinner, healed the sick, raised the dead, died on a cross and saved humanity, rose from the dead, destroyed the works of the devil, ascended into heaven and is now seated at the right hand of the Father.

Now, you may be thinking that I don't know God that intimately, and so you may be reluctant to step out in faith to fulfill your God-given destiny. In the story below, we will demonstrate that you are more than enough right now, and that you are well able to do what your heart and soul desires.

THE STORY OF TWO COUSINS WHO CHANGED THE WORLD

Once upon a time there were two cousins, Brendan and Quinlan, who were born under seemingly impossible circumstances—one to an elderly couple, the other to a teenage girl.

They grew up together and, to their amazement, had similar dreams of being motivational speakers. As they grew older, the elder cousin, Brendan, decided it was time for him to take his show on the road. So he packed and moved to Las Vegas.

Brendan was a smooth brother. He was health conscious and fashion conscious. His favorite outfit combination was fur and leather, the kind Rick James or Eddie Murphy would wear.

Every time he went on stage he was on point. He would mesmerize his audiences with charisma and charm.

Here are some excerpts from his "Change Your Mind" speech:

"I am the one you've been waiting for. As a matter of fact, I am the one your mama's been waiting for. This is not the time to play the waiting game. The government you seek is now here. Change your mind. This is the time to be strong. There is no room for the weak. Be the change you seek. We are the change we seek."

It was not long after when people from all over the country began to take notice. They would come from near and far to see and to hear him speak. Soon he had a huge physical following, from the common man to government and religious officials. His Twitter and Facebook following grew daily. No one needed to ask what's trending. He was the trend.

One day while on stage, he remembered his cousin, Quinlan, and the common dream they shared. So he began to tell the people about this cousin who was way better than he was. He would say, "My cousin is so perfect that if he were to ask me to carry his shoes, I would have to say no for fear of messing them up."

Not too long thereafter, Quinlan showed up to one of Brendan's seminars. Brendan recognized him, brought him on stage and introduced him to his audience. While on stage, a conversation ensued between them:

Brendan: So, Quinlan, what brought you to Vegas?
Quinlan: You are the man. I came to see you. I would like to be mentored by you.

Brendan: Me mentor you? No way! I am the one who should be your apprentice. You are joking, right?

Quinlan: No, I am serious. I am so ready! Remember? We were born for this!

Brendan reluctantly agreed and decided to initiate him right there on stage. At the end of the initiation, Quinlan glowed like a disco ball. As the audience stared at him in awe, a voice from heaven echoed these words: "This is my beloved son in whom I am well pleased. Listen to him."

Before Quinlan ever did anything, His father made it known to the world that he was pleased with his son. Today that voice still speaks.

This is my beloved (son/daughter) {your name} in whom I am well pleased. Listen to (him/her).

You are loved

You are valued

You are competent

Worthy is the lamb that was slain, and worthy are they for whom he was slain.

YOU ARE WORTHY.

WHERE TO GO FROM HERE

Should you have questions or comments for me, suggestions for future material, or tips, feel free to e-mail me at info@thechrisgrant.com.

I am available for speaking engagements and am accepting applications for my coaching programs. To book Chris Grant, please visit www.thechrisgrant.com.